THE
GRAPES OF WRATH

NOTES

including
- *Life and Background*
- *Introduction*
- *General Plot Summary*
- *List of Characters*
- *Chapter Summaries and Commentaries*
- *Notes on General Meaning and Style*
- *Character Analysis*
- *Examination Questions*
- *Selected Bibliography*

by
James L. Roberts, Ph.D.
Department of English
University of Nebraska

INCORPORATED

LINCOLN, NEBRASKA 68501

Editor

Gary Carey, M.A.
University of Colorado

Consulting Editor

James L. Roberts, Ph.D.
Department of English
University of Nebraska

ISBN 0-8220-0542-5
© Copyright 1965
by
Cliffs Notes, Inc.
All Rights Reserved
Printed in U.S.A.

1999 Printing

Cliffs Notes, Inc.   Lincoln, Nebraska

CONTENTS

THE GRAPES OF WRATH

LIFE AND BACKGROUND

John Steinbeck is the type of author who likes to know his material first hand. He is not content to narrate a story which has no basis in fact. Thus most of his works take place in California and deal with subjects which he thoroughly understands.

Steinbeck's father settled in California shortly after the American Civil War. John Steinbeck was born in Salinas on February 27, 1902. His mother was a school teacher in the public school in Salinas. Steinbeck grew up in this beautiful fertile California valley. From this valley, he found the materials for most of his novels. His imagination was kindled toward writing at a very early age partly because his mother, the school teacher, read to him from the famous literature of the world.

During his formative years, he played various sports in high school, worked at various jobs, and wandered around the countryside observing the phenomena of nature. He entered Stanford University in 1920, and even though he remained until 1925, he never graduated. In fact, he earned very few credits. He did, however, contribute some material to the Stanford literary magazine, both poems and short stories.

During his years at Stanford and immediately after his departure, Steinbeck worked at a variety of jobs. He went to New York in 1925, but found it unsuitable for his temperament. He returned to California, and between odd jobs, he began writing his novels. His first novel appeared in 1929.

In preparation for writing his novels, Steinbeck would often live, work and be with the people about whom he was to write. Thus, in preparation for writing *The Grapes of Wrath,* Steinbeck went to Oklahoma, joined some migrants and rode with them to California. Once in California, he stayed with these migrants, living with them in Hoovervilles, joining them in their search for work, and attempting as much as possible, to come to terms with these people's essential characteristics. Leaving them, he made several trips to various camps to observe first-hand the living and working conditions of these migrants. He wrote some short pieces for the *San Francisco News* in which he described the plight of these people, and pleaded for a more tolerant approach in the handling of these migrants. These articles, however, were not very effective. It was only when he molded his raw experiences into the form of a novel that effects were achieved.

For his total body of works, Mr. Steinbeck was awarded the Nobel Prize for literature in 1962, the highest honor in the field of literature.

THE NOVEL OF PROTEST

CRITICAL ACCEPTANCE

The Grapes of Wrath has most often been considered a novel of protest or a social document. When the novel first appeared, the public began to take sides over its value. It was seldom discussed as a work of art, but instead, the subject matter was debated as to whether the facts were falsified, and whether the situation could possibly be this bad. From the religious viewpoint, it was attacked as obscene. It never had a chance to be evaluated as a work of art.

There were particularly vehement attacks against the book by the people of Oklahoma and California. The citizens of Oklahoma resented the fact that the people were depicted as *Okies* and denied the implications that Oklahoma is a dust bowl where it is impossible to grow crops. An Oklahoma congressman went on record maintaining that the book is a "black, infernal creation of a twisted, distorted mind." In California there appeared numerous pamphlets proving that John Steinbeck had written nothing but black lies. Within six months, there had been more public response to his novel than to any novel in American history with the possible exception of *Uncle Tom's Cabin*.

Steinbeck, however, was not without his defenders. Ministers, university professors, sociologists, and government agents testified to the accuracy of Steinbeck's portrayal. Magazines such as *Life* ran feature stories on the plight of the migrants, and before the novel was made into a movie, the director sent men into the field to verify the accuracy of the novel, and his agents reported that conditions were much worse than had been reported by Steinbeck.

The furor raised by the publication of this novel has now passed into history. Many of the attacks were made by people ashamed of the desperate plight of the migrants, and ashamed of the way American citizens were treated by fellow Americans, but the immediate social situation is now past history. The reader today is not so much concerned with the sociological aspect of the novel. He should be aware that Steinbeck was telling an accurate story, but the plight of the migrants has virtually faded from the memory of the American people, leaving us free to evaluate the novel on artistic grounds.

The only point that Steinbeck was attacked on, that is still relevant today is the social philosophy advocated in the novel. Since his attackers accused him of being a communist because of this philosophy, we must consider this aspect of the novel in interpreting the exact nature of that philosophy. Today, to the more rational mind, we see that it is not so much a communistic philosophy as it is an Emersonian view. Emerson had maintained that every man comes from a great Oversoul and in death returns to that Oversoul. His ultimate conclusion involved the holiness or divinity of every man. This is essentially the same belief advocated by Jim Casy. This is transcendentalism and not communism, but the American public has needed the lapse of time to fully understand and appreciate the full meaning of this great novel of social protest, which is also a great work of art.

STRUCTURE

Steinbeck once said that the plight of the migrants was something impersonal and distant. Even though the American people knew about these people, they did not understand the nature of the entire situation. He felt that the American people could never really sympathize with these migrants merely from reading about and hearing about their general plight. Therefore, he decided to tell the story of one family. He thought that if the public could become intimately acquainted with one family, then the entire situation would be better understood. Thus he wrote *The Grapes of Wrath* so that the public could personally get to know one family of migrants.

In telling the story, there seemed to be a lot of material left over. He wanted to tell a moving narrative about the Joads, but the narrative alone did not cover the entire picture. He therefore inserted chapters which spoke of the general picture of the society with which the Joads were involved. Thus we have the intercalary chapters, i.e., chapters which are not about the Joads, but about the background of the dust bowl, about the highway that leads from Oklahoma to California, about selling property, about the ownership of land in California, etc. These chapters present the plight in a general sense. They act as support for the narrative, and they reflect many aspects of the Joad narrative. The specific purpose of each chapter is discussed in a commentary after the chapter, but the general purpose is to present the social background against which the Joad's plight is seen, and also to give historical information which led to the present situation.

None of the main characters in the narrative portion of the novel appear in the intercalary chapters. But the reader should be aware of the close relationship between the intercalary and the narrative chapters. While the intercalary chapters fulfill the functions mentioned above, there is still artistic interweaving between these chapters. As pointed out in the *Commentaries,* the intercalary chapters serve many artistic and symbolic functions. Sometimes they are a comment on some action and sometimes they foreshadow actions that will occur later in the novel.

This technique of inserting general chapters in between the narrative chapters is not new with Steinbeck. It has been used by other famous writers, such as Fielding (*Tom Jones*) and Tolstoi (*War and Peace*). Steinbeck's successful handling of this technique contributes greatly to the success of this novel.

GENERAL PLOT SUMMARY

Tom Joad is hitchhiking home after being released from the state prison on parole. He has served four years of a seven year sentence. He catches a ride with a truck driver who takes him to the road which leads to his family's farm. As he is walking the rest of the way, he meets Jim Casy, an itinerant preacher. Casy explains that he has been away for some time trying to figure out some things, and has decided that since all things are holy, he need not be a preacher any more but just live with the people because the people are holy. They go together to Tom's place. When they arrive, they find that the place is deserted. They can't understand it. It looks as though all the neighboring farms are deserted. Soon they see someone coming. It is Muley Graves who tells them that Tom's folks are at his Uncle John's. Jim and Tom sleep in the fields that night and walk on to Uncle John's the next day.

When they arrive, they find the Joads making preparations for a trip. It is explained to Tom that the banks and large companies closed out all the small farmers, and now most of them are heading to California where there is supposed to be work. They sell all of their belongings, but get only eighteen dollars for them. Casy joins them, because he has to be where the people are. When they are about ready to leave, Grampa Joad doesn't want to leave. They have to dope him in order to get him away. When they stop on the first night of the journey west, Grampa has a stroke and dies immediately. The Joads, who have stopped next to some more migrants, the Wilsons, borrow a quilt from the Wilsons and bury Grampa. They then fix the Wilson's broken-down car, and the two families begin the trip together. Just as they reach California, Mrs. Wilson becomes so sick that she can't go any further, and the Joads give them some money and food and leave them.

During the entire trip, Granma Joad has been getting sicker and sicker. As they begin the trip across the great desert at night, Ma Joad realizes that Granma is dying. She explains to the old woman that the family must get across the desert because they are about out of money. Granma dies early in the night. When a guard stops them, Ma Joad tells the guard that they must get to a doctor because Granma is sick. The guard looks and lets them pass. Ma tells the family to drive on, and in the morning when they are safely across, she tells the family that Granma is dead. They have to leave her to be buried a pauper because they don't have enough money for a funeral.

They arrive in a place where many other migrants are camping. Even though it is filthy and disorderly, they stop. But the men are unable to find work. A contractor comes through looking for workers, and when a friend of Tom's asks what they are paying, the friend is accused of being a "red" and is arrested. A fight ensues, and the sheriff tells the people that the whole camp will be burned. The Joads pack up and leave. They find a vacancy in a government camp which is protected from the sheriff. Here there is law and order, but the Joads are still unable to find work. Soon they are out of money and food and must move on in search of work.

They hear of work in a peach orchard. When they arrive, they are escorted into the camp by policemen. There are many men standing outside the camp, some yelling and waving. The Joads begin picking peaches immediately so they can have something to eat that night. Later Tom slips outside to investigate the situation involving the yelling men. He finds his friend, Jim Casy, who has been in prison, and Casy tells Tom that they are striking against the owners of the orchard who cut the wages in half. While they are talking, some men come looking for Casy who is apparently the leader of the strike. The men advance on Casy and immediately kill him. Tom becomes infuriated and kills one of the men. He flees and gets back to the camp, but has to hide because his nose is broken. The Joads' wages are cut in half the next day because the strike is broken. They leave and find a place where they can pick cotton and where Tom can hide in a nearby thicket.

One of the Joad children gets into a fight and threatens to call her brother Tom, bragging that he has killed a man. Ma hears about the child's threat and goes to Tom and tells him that he must leave. Tom is going to carry on with the work that Casy was doing, and he takes a little money from Ma Joad and leaves.

As soon as the cotton picking is over, the rains set in. Just as the Joads are thinking about leaving, Rose of Sharon, the daughter, goes into labor pains. Pa and some other men try to build an embankment to keep out the rising water. But the embankment collapses. The baby is born, but it is dead. The water continues to rise, and comes into the boxcar where they are living. Pa Joad builds a platform inside the boxcar where they stay for two more days.

As soon as the rains slacken a little, Ma Joad says that the family must find some drier place. Carrying the children on their backs, they wade through the water until come to the highway. Down the road they find a barn with some dry hay. They also discover a man dying from starvation. The man's son tells them that his father hasn't eaten for six days. The Joads have no money and no food. Ma suggests to Rose of Sharon that she feed the dying man from her breast which Rose of Sharon gladly does.

CAST OF CHARACTERS

Note: for a fuller discussion of the main characters, see the section at the end on *Character Analysis*.

PA JOAD
A tenant farmer who has just lost his farm as a result of the Oklahoma dust destroying the crops. He is taking his family to California where he hopes to get work.

MA JOAD
The strong, determined wife and mother who is the guiding or controlling member of the family. She holds the family together.

GRAMPA AND GRANMA
The grandparents who originally settled the forty acres which Pa Joad has just lost.

NOAH JOAD
The oldest son who was somewhat injured at birth when Pa Joad had to perform the delivery. He moves rather slowly and quietly.

TOM JOAD
The second son who killed a man four years ago in a fight and who has been paroled after four years in the state prison.

ROSE OF SHARON
The daughter who is married to Connie. She is expecting a baby and dreams of a nice place to live in California.

AL JOAD
The sixteen-year old son who is interested only in cars and girls.

CONNIE
Rose of Sharon's husband who deserts her after they reach California.

RUTHIE and WINFIELD JOAD
Ruthie and Winfield are the two youngest. Ruthie is just twelve and Winfield is ten.

JIM CASY
Casy was once a preacher, but has decided to give it up because he has found that everything is holy, and man needs no preacher to say this. He goes along with the Joads to California.

IVY and SARAH (SAIRY) WILSON
A couple that the Joads meet when they first begin their journey West. The Joads fix the Wilson's car and help them across the country.

MR. and MRS. WAINWRIGHT
The family who live in the opposite end of the boxcar during the last part of the novel.

AGNES WAINWRIGHT
Their young daughter who becomes engaged to Al Joad.

MULEY GRAVES
A neighbor to the Joads who refuses to leave his land after he lost it and who is living wild and sneaky like some animal.

EZRA HUSTON
Chairman of the central committee in the government camp in California.

WILLIE EATON
The man in charge of the entertainment committee and who directs the actions against the rioters.

JULE VITELA
A half-breed Indian, whom Tom meets at the government camp.

CHAPTER I

Summary
In the red and gray country of Oklahoma, the last of the rain came in early May. Even that was only enough to cause small droplets to appear. Then the weeds began to turn color to guard against the onslaught of the sun. The corn began to fade and dry up. When June was half gone, a few drops of rain fell, but it only made the dust on the corn seem freckled. Soon it became necessary to tie handkerchiefs over one's nose for protection against the dust. At night the dust failed to settle so that the stars could not pierce the dust. Little lines of dust crept into the houses even though they were all padded.

The men just stood and looked at the ruined corn. The women would come out and look at the men to see if they would break. The "women and children knew deep in themselves that no misfortune was too great to bear if their men were whole."

Commentary
The first chapter, short as it is, presents the essential background situation which will cause the great migration toward California. Here we see the land being turned into a dust bowl, the crops being ruined, and the men idle.

Chapters of general importance will be interspersed throughout the novel. Generally, Steinbeck will have a chapter of narration followed by a chapter of indirect comment or a general situation which suggests something about the personal tragedy of the main characters. These inserted chapters are called intercalary chapters.

The idleness of the men suggested at the end of the chapter and the way in which the women watch their men will be one of the central motifs throughout the novel. The women can keep going as long as their men don't give up. Thus later, Ma Joad will intentionally goad her husband in order to test him, in order to see if he has given up.

CHAPTER II

Summary

A man walking along the highway crossed over to a roadside cafe where a huge transport truck was parked. He noticed the "No Riders" sign on the truck, but he sat down on the running board and waited anyway. He was dressed in a cheap new suit of clothes and new shoes. While waiting, he unlaced his new shoes. Inside the restaurant, he could hear music blaring from a machine. Soon, the truck driver came out and the man asked him for a ride. The driver pointed to the "No Riders" sign, but the man said that some drivers will be a "good guy even if some rich bastard makes him carry a sticker." The driver thought a minute and told the man to hide until they came around the corner and then he could climb in.

When they were down the road, the driver started talking at random about a number of things. He began to ask the man all kinds of questions. When the man tells him that he is returning to his "old man's" forty acre place, the driver is surprised that someone with only forty acres still has a place which hasn't been taken over by a "cat." The man explains that he has been away for four years, and then gets rather angry at all the questioning and tells the driver his name is Tom Joad. The driver tries to explain that he gets lonesome driving all day and didn't mean any offense by the questions, but he just feels the need to talk. He talks some more and tells how he is planning on studying fingerprints. Then Tom accuses the driver of trying to snoop into everyone's business, and Tom confesses that he has been to McAlester, the state prison, for four years. He was convicted of manslaughter and sentenced for seven years, but he got out early for good behavior. By this time, Tom is at the road leading to the farm.

Commentary

While there are many symbolic passages and events in this novel, the central emphasis is on plot and the development of the central situation. It will be through a dramatic telling of the struggles of the Joad family that the central meaning of the novel will be revealed. Therefore, the plot summary and the situation developing in the story line carry the burden of the meaning of this great novel. This chapter begins to set up certain elements of the central story. Tom, who has been in prison, will become a mainstay of the family, but because of his record, he will also become somewhat of a burden. That is, he will not be free to act as he would like.

One of the central motifs is suggested by the sign on the truck. The "No Riders" sign implies for Tom that the "rich bastards" are the opposite of the good guy — that the rich are out to destroy the poor. This begins to set the tone for the episodes with the land owners both in California and now in Oklahoma.

The driver's surprise that Tom's family still has a farm presents in advance the essential predicament. Actually Tom's family has already been shoved out by one of the big cats (machines which were used in farming that were big enough to knock down one of the small houses found on the tenant farms). The episode with the truck driver is often carried over into the bulk of the novel. As the Joads travel along, they will often run into scenes involving truck drivers and stop-over restaurants. Ma Joad says at the end, when a poor person wants something, he had best go for help to one of his own kind. Thus it was that Tom was even able to get a ride with the truck driver in the first place.

CHAPTER III

Summary

The concrete highway lay amid a mat of dried grass. A few grasshoppers were to be seen. A land turtle approached the highway and slowly and laboriously climbed the embankment. After many frantic efforts, he finally reaches the top and slowly begins the long and arduous crossing. A car driven by a forty-year old woman passed by. She swerved to miss the turtle. A few minutes later, a light truck came down the road driven by a young man. He swerved to hit it. He clipped the edge of the shell and flipped the turtle off the highway. It landed on its back, and had to struggle for some time before it could turn itself back over. Then it slowly proceeded on its way.

Commentary

Often in Steinbeck's writing, there is an implication that man is a victim of a hostile universe, that he has little or no control over his destiny. Thus the presentation of the slow moving turtle trying to fulfill his destination, and being hindered by ants, hills, oat seeds under his shell, and finally, by the dangerous traffic offers a rather bitter analogy to the predicament of man. And throughout the novel, the Joad family meets with such hardships, but as the turtle refused to be swayed from his purpose, so the Joads will continue to struggle with great fortitude.

Passages such as these attest to Steinbeck's greatness as a realistic and symbolic writer. Steinbeck bases his presentation on a highly realistic rendition of facts. The description of the turtle is accurate in the finest degree. Yet in the very realism of the description, we have suggested the realistic view of this hostile world.

CHAPTER IV

Summary

Tom watches the truck drive off and then turns toward home. He notices the thickness of the dust. Close by is a land turtle. He picks it up and plans to take it to one of the kids. As he walks along, he notices a person sitting under a tree. Tom approaches and speaks. The man recognizes Tom as Old Tom Joad's son. He explains that he is the preacher who baptized Tom, but says that Tom was too busy pulling some girl's pigtails to be bothered with baptism. He is the Reverend Jim Casy, but he is no longer a preacher. He doesn't have the call anymore. Tom offers him a drink which Jim accepts. Jim Casy then goes into a long explanation of how he lost his calling to be a preacher. He explains that he used to meet some girl during the meetings and then afterwards he would take her out on the grass and sleep with her. Now he knew that wasn't right so he went off to think about it. For years now he has been thinking it over and now realizes that there "aint no sin and there ain't no virtue." There is nothing but the actions of men and this is what is important. Human beings are more important than the abstract concepts involved in religion. Thus, man needs to live and doesn't need preaching because just living is holy.

Tom picks up his turtle and is about to go. Casy asks him how his father is. Tom explains he hasn't been around for over four years, and Casy wonders why. Tom explains that he got in a fight with a man four years ago, and the man stuck a knife in him and Tom hit the man with a shovel. He was sentenced for manslaughter and served four of his seven year sentence. Casy wonders if Tom is ashamed. Tom tells him that he had to defend himself and he is not ashamed. Casy wonders about the prison life, and Tom explains that they eat regularly and even have a shower bath everyday. He tells how one man was out and couldn't stand it because he was hungry all the time and never knew where he was going to eat, so he stole a car so that he could be sent back to the prison.

As Tom is leaving, Casy wonders if he could join him. He would like to speak with Old Tom. Tom tells him that he is welcome because his family always thought well of the preacher. On the way, Tom tells him a story about his Uncle John who would kill a shoat and eat all he could at one time and then leave the rest. As they approach the house, both of them notice that something is wrong. Then they realize that no one is there.

Commentary

Often we will find some type of connection between the chapter of general comment and those of narrative comment. Thus, at the beginning of this chapter, Tom picks up a turtle. This does not mean that it is the same turtle that was described in the last chapter, but the reader will often find this connecting suggestion.

Chapter IV is devoted to introducing the preacher, Jim Casy. His slow and laborious intellectual realization is central to the novel. Even though it took him over four years to come to this realization, yet it is maintained throughout the novel. That is, it is not abstract concepts that matter so much as it is the actions of human beings. Thus, Ma Joad functions in the novel not as some abstract concept, but as a living individual. And the plight of the Joad family is not some abstract problem for America to face, but it is a living problem involving definite human beings. Thus we come to Steinbeck's great purpose of the novel. These people are not just a group of undesirable "Okies" but they are living human beings who are being starved to death in this particular American society.

Casy will be the contemplative man for some time yet. His thoughts will not be put into action until they reach California. He functions also as a contrast to Tom Joad. We see here at first that Tom is somewhat self-centered. He is thinking mainly of himself, but Casy is trying to work out something for greater humanity. This will become clearer as the novel progresses.

CHAPTER V

Summary
Sometimes the owners of the land came to the tenant family with a sense of anger because they hated what they had to do; other owners came with a sense of grief or kindness because they too hated what they had to do. All of them, owner and tenant, seemed to be caught in something larger than themselves. Then the owner explained that the tenant system wouldn't work anymore. The tenant suggested maybe another year would bring better crops, or maybe if they rotated the crops it would be better. They reminded the owner that their grandpas settled the land and furthermore, they have no place to go. They can't take smaller shares because the youngsters don't have enough to eat as it is now. But the owner only said that the tenants would have to leave.

Then the tractor hired by the bank or corporation would come over the land plowing a straight line and knocking down anything that stood in the way of a good straight line. At noon, the driver of the iron machine would take off his goggles and eat. He would look strange with dust settled on parts of his face and with lines where the goggles fit.

At noon a tractor driver stops by a tenant house and tells the tenant that he would have to knock the tenant's house down that afternoon because it is obstructing the straight line that he must plow. The tenant recognizes the driver as being a neighbor's boy. He wonders why the boy does this to his own people. The driver tells him that his family doesn't have any food and his kids have never had shoes, and this company pays three dollars a day. The tenant farmer can't stand the idea of being pushed off property that used to be his. He threatens to shoot the driver, but the driver tells him that he would just be hanged and another driver would be pushing the house down before he was hanged. The tenant farmer wants to kill someone, but the driver gets his orders from the bank and the bank is ordered by someone else, so there is no one to attack.

Commentary

This chapter is the abstract or allegorical conflict between the tenant farmer and the banks. This is the great generalized conflict involving all the people of this sort. This chapter, then, presents the general situation which will in turn become personal when we see the Joad family caught up in the identical conflict. And whereas the tenant farmer threatens to shoot the driver, later we find out that Grandpa actually did take a shot at a driver. As the tenant farmer bemoans the loss of property which was settled by his own grandfather, so the Joads feel the loss of the land settled by their forefathers. The actual leaving of the land is directly correlated later with Grandpa's death.

CHAPTER VI

Summary

As Tom and Jim Casy approach the Joad house, they see that it has been knocked in at one corner. Going to the well, they can't understand why it is dry. The barn is empty and the house is pushed all out of shape. Tom knows that something is wrong, but he can't put his finger on it. When Tom sees a cat wandering around, he finally realizes that there are no neighbors either. If the Joads had moved, the other neighbors would have come and taken the lumber and other things, but nothing has been disturbed, thus there must not be any one left in the country. Tom then unwraps the land turtle and lets it loose. Immediately, the turtle heads toward the southwest.

Suddenly, they notice someone coming down the road, but he is covered with so much dust that they can't identify him. Finally Tom recognizes him as Muley Graves. They yell at him, and frighten him, but he comes on to them, and recognizes Tom. Muley immediately tells Tom that Old Tom was worried because they were leaving and couldn't let young Tom know about it. He goes into a long explanation before Tom is able to force him to come to the point and tell where the Joads are. Muley says that they have all moved in with Tom's Uncle John. They have been chopping cotton to get enough money to buy a car and head out for California.

Tom wants to go to Muley's place for the night since his Uncle John's place is so far away. Muley explains that he has already been pushed off his place, and his family has gone to California, but he could not leave the land that his own pa settled. Tom wants to know who pushed him off. Muley is not able to explain it well, but it seems that some large land company bought up the land and can only make a profit by doing away with the tenants and replacing them with tractors and day laborers.

By this time, Tom is ravenously hungry and asks Muley where and how he eats. Muley pulls out a cottontail rabbit and a jack rabbit. Tom wonders if Muley is going to share and Muley explains that a man doesn't have a choice; when he has food and another doesn't, a man just has to share. By the time they build a fire, cook and eat the rabbit, they notice approaching car lights in the distance. Muley explains that they have to hide or else they will get into trouble for trespassing. Tom doesn't want to hide, especially on his own father's land, but Muley reminds Tom that he has a parole and must not get into trouble. They hide while the deputy comes looking around, puts out the fire, throws out a searchlight and finally leaves.

Muley offers to show them where to sleep for the night. He leads them to a small cave in the bank. Tom recognizes it as one he partially dug years ago. Tom refuses to sleep in the cave, preferring the open night. Casy maintains that he won't be able to sleep because he has got to work out some things in his mind.

Commentary

This chapter takes the general statements of the last intercalary chapter and makes them specific. Whereas the last chapter was written in general terms about the plight of the tenant farmers, we now see that the Joad's house has been pushed in, and we see what happens to one individual who refuses to move. Muley Graves becomes a living, dead man. He has become more of an animal than a human being, and he is able to sustain himself only by adopting animal habits. Here, also, Tom frees the turtle which immediately continues on its way toward the southwest, the same direction in which the Joads will go.

When Muley shares his meager meal with Tom and Casy, he comments that "if a fella's got somepin' to eat an another fella's hungry—why, the first fella ain't got no choice." As with the actions of the Joads later, we see that these people exist because each is willing to share and help the other. They don't understand their actions. It is up to Jim Casy to verbalize the actions into the belief that all people are just a part of one great being.

The full meaning of Tom's parole comes to him as he realizes that he cannot act as a free man. His parole modifies his actions, and later in California, we see the same type of restraining force preventing Tom from following his natural instincts.

It is both ironic and a bit of foreshadowing that Tom refuses to sleep in the cave that Muley leads them to. In the last episodes of the novel, Tom is forced to hide in a cave where he lives for several days, and is only too glad to find this refuge.

CHAPTER VII

Summary

Used cars are lined up on lots and salesmen are selling them as rapidly as possible. There seems to be a larger profit and turnover in used cars than in new ones. The owner always tries to take out the good battery before he makes delivery, and if the gears or transmission are making a lot of noise, he will pour sawdust inside to cut down on the noise. The used car dealer likes to deal with the tenant farmer who knows nothing about cars and who will sign notes at high interest rates. And if something goes wrong with a car, it is easy to ignore a tenant farmer's complaint. And besides, they take the cars and leave the country.

Commentary

This chapter again presents a general social situation in which the Joads will later be involved. They will have to have a used car in which to go to California.

Taken separately, these intercalary chapters present the social situation which causes the narrative situation. The first chapter presented the dust bowl being created. Then the last intercalary chapter (five) presented the foreclosing of mortgages which forced the farmer to immigrate. In his preparation for leaving, he must buy a car, and this chapter will show the type of situation he will confront when he attempts to buy his car.

CHAPTER VIII

Summary

The night is still dark when Muley awakens Tom and Casy and tells them that he is going. So Tom and Casy begin the walk to Uncle John's house. Casy asks about Uncle John and Tom tells him how strange and different Uncle John is. He was once married and when his wife was pregnant, she got a pain in her stomach one night and asked for a doctor. Uncle John told her she just had a "bellyache" from eating too much. By the next day at noon, she was out of her mind and later that day she died. Uncle John never got over it and ever since has been a little strange. Whenever he is around kids, he does things like slipping them gum or candy.

As they approach Uncle John's, Tom notices that all the furniture is stacked out in the yard. He realizes that his family is about to pull out. He tells Casy not to say anything and they walk quietly up to the house. Old Tom is working on the car. Tom speaks to him, but for a minute Old Tom is not aware of who it is. As soon as he recognizes Tom, he wants to know if Tom has broken out of the jail. Tom tells him about the parole.

Old Tom explains that they were about to leave for California and that they were going to write him a letter. But Ma has been taking it rather hard, because she was afraid that she would never see him again. Pa told Tom to come into the kitchen but not to say anything to Ma. Once inside the house, Pa asked Ma if two strangers could have a bite of breakfast. At first Ma merely said to send them in and paid no attention to them. Then she slowly recognized Tom. Her first concern was also as to whether he had broken out. Then she moved close to him so that she could feel the "soundness of his muscles." She felt his cheek and stroked him. Then she recovered and welcomed him home. She sent Pa down to the barn to get Grampa and Granma. She explained to Tom that Grampa and Granma sleep in the barn because they have to get up so much during the night that they disturb everyone else.

While everyone is gone, Ma asks Tom if he is mad, because she once knew Purty Boy Floyd and he wasn't "mean-mad" until they put him in prison and made him become "mean-mad." Tom assures her that he is alright. About this time, Granma comes up to the house shouting "pu-raise Gawd fur vittory." Grampa is following trying to button his pants. They race each other across the yard. Behind them moving slowly and evenly is Noah. When Noah was born, Pa was alone with Ma and became frightened and tried to pull and twist Noah into birth. The midwife arrived later and tried to push Noah's head back into shape.

Granma and Grampa were both real pleased to see Tom; they tell how Tom should have killed that fellow and shouldn't have gone to jail. When breakfast is served, Granma insists upon having the preacher say grace. But Casy explains that he is not a preacher any longer. Granma insists on a prayer. Casy merely recites how he went out alone and thought about things. "I got thinkin' how we was holy when we was one thing, an' mankin' was holy when it was one thing." At the end of this long talk, he quits, but everyone waits until he returns and says *amen.*

After breakfast, Pa shows Tom the truck that Al, the sixteen-year old brother, had helped them buy. Al had worked for a company and knew something about cars. But he hasn't been home for some time because he is too busy "tom-cattin' hisself to death." Tom asks about the rest of the family. The two kids, Ruthie and Winfield, who are twelve and ten, went with Uncle John to sell some household equipment. Rose of Sharon is married and is going to have a baby.

About this time, they notice Al coming up the road. He is swaggering until he sees Tom. Al had gained a certain amount of notoriety simply by being the brother of a person who had killed a man, and he wanted to imitate Tom. Thus when he saw that Tom was the quiet and brooding type, Al dropped his swagger and tried to imitate Tom's stance. He was real pleased that Tom wanted to shake hands, and asked Tom if he wanted to ride into Sallisaw, but Tom reminded him that they would be together on the road.

Commentary

We are introduced in this chapter to Ma Joad, the bulwark and mainstay of the Joad family. She is the one most concerned with keeping the family together. She is the one who seems to transcend the personal and individual and looks at all of humanity. When there is happiness, all turn to her to gauge their reactions. She never shows hurt or fear. She is the strength and comfort of the family and she suppresses her own feelings for the sake of the entire family.

When Tom comes to her, she is radiant because she was afraid that she was losing one member of the family. She goes to him and feels his strength and his face as a blind man might. This image is particularly strong, since in their last meeting, she is in the darkness of the cave and reaches and feels him in the same manner as here.

If Ma Joad represents the immediate family here, then Casy's thinking is reaching the point of showing that all of humanity is a part of one thing, is one great family in itself. Ma puts this theory in practice in the way she so readily helps others. And early in the novel, she verbalizes for us the idea of man joining together against outside forces. This will become a dominant motif later in California. "They say there's a hundred thousand of us shoved out. If we was all mad the same way, Tommy — they wouldn't hunt nobody down."

Each member of the family inquires immediately if Tom has broken out. Thus, his position will often hamper the family.

This chapter presents the first hints of the "grapes" which stand symbolically for a new and better way of life. No one now knows that the grapes of hope will become the grapes of wrath.

CHAPTER IX

Summary
Families of tenant people sift through their collection of property and memories, searching to find what can be sold. They are leaving for California and cannot take the stuff with them. They have to sell. There was a seeder that cost thirty-eight dollars and the man got only two dollars for it. But he couldn't take it with him to California. The buyer would pretend that he wasn't interested in their junk at any price and then the tenant farmers realized that they had to sell at any price. But the buyers didn't know that the junk they were buying was the junk that life is made from. Defeated by a system of buying and selling that they didn't understand, the men would trudge slowly back to the farmyards and there report to the women on their failure. Then the women would start sorting through the old memories, the collected items of the past: the book that grandfather read, or the souvenir that some aunt brought from some fair. But it all had to go. There was no room on the truck for sentimental items. Then as the time for departure came, there was a frenzied air of activity. Everyone was frantic to get the trip underway.

Commentary

These intercalary chapters always connect some action of the Joads with some larger actions. They remind us constantly that the plight of the Joads is not an individual plight, but is symtomatic of a whole society. Thus we have the interconnecting links. In the last intercalary chapter, there was the purchase of the automobile. Then in Chapters IX and XI, we are given information about the Joad's purchase of a used car. This chapter, Chapter IX, describes the generalized families who must sell all their goods at absurd prices, report back to the women, and then become frenzied about leaving. In the last chapter we found out that Uncle John had already left with the team and wagon, and now Pa and Al are about to leave with the extra household things. Furthermore, in the next chapter, we find Pa dreading telling Ma how little he was able to get for their property. And finally, after the decision is made to go, the entire Joad family makes this frenzied effort to get away. Thus, the intercalary chapters contribute to making the novel a larger social document and suggest some of the personal problems the main characters will have.

CHAPTER X

Summary

When the truck has gone, Tom wanders around the places he remembers. Then his mother approaches him and wonders if things will really be so nice in California as the handbills and the people say they are. She tells him that she doesn't have the faith anymore that she used to have. Tom explains that the only way he was able to endure prison life was to live from day to day and not think about things in the future. He tells of a person he knew from California who said that the fruit pickers lived in dirty camps, got low wages, and hardly enough to eat. But Ma has confidence in the handbill that she saw.

Grampa gets up from where he has been sleeping, and Ma has to go over and button him up. He is annoyed, but keeps thinking about the grapes he will eat once he gets to California. Casy comes in and wonders if he will be able to go along with the Joads. He says that he has to be with the people. Ma assures him that he would be welcome, but first it must be decided by the menfolk in a council. Casy says he is not going to preach anymore, but just wants to be with the people, because that in itself is holy.

In the late afternoon, Pa and the family arrive with the truck. He is tired and "angry and sad" because he has gotten only eighteen dollars for everything that the family had possessed. And he knows that Ma is going to be disappointed. But he didn't know what to do because the buyer pretended that he didn't want the stuff at any price.

Tom greets the rest of the family, and then the family "government went into session." Al explains his reasons for choosing this car, and is very pleased when Tom tells him that he has done a good job. Tom then brings up the subject of taking Casy along. During the council meeting, Casy has respectfully withdrawn to the rear of the house. Pa wonders if they will have room and enough food for an extra mouth, but Ma reminds him that the Joads have never turned anyone down. They are already too crowded and one more won't hurt matters. Once it is decided to take Casy, they invite him to join in the family conference and help decide matters.

The subject of when to leave is next. They have to slaughter and salt down two pigs and pack all of their stuff before they go. They can't slaughter the meat during the day because it is too warm. So they decide to break up and slaughter the pigs immediately. After this is accomplished, they realize that on the next day they won't have too much to do, so they decide to pitch in and work all night so that they can leave at dawn. Then there is a frenzied effort to get everything packed. Ma is busy salting down the pork, but Casy tells her he can do that. Ma protests that it is woman's work, but Casy says that there is too much work to break it down into "men's or women's work." She instructs the men as to what must go, and then she goes to sort through her private souvenirs. She brings out the old box, filled with clippings, including the newspaper account of Tom's trial, and filled with remembrances like photographs, letters, and braids of hair. She selects a few items and throws the rest into the fire.

As they are about ready to leave, **Muley Graves** comes up to say goodby. He asks them to tell his family that he is alright. The Joads offer to take him along. He would like to go, but just can't bring himself to leave the country. At this time, Grampa arrives and says that he is not going. He tells them that he will live just like Muley is living, and "I'll just stay right where I b'long." Tom takes the family aside for a conference. They all agree that Grampa can't stay, but they can't force him because he would hurt himself. So they decide to give him some kind of sleeping medicine that Ma once had for one of the kids. They give Grampa a big dose in his coffee and soon he is sound asleep. They load Grampa on the truck, ask Muley if he could look after the dogs, and give him the chickens that they are leaving.

Commentary

The first note of doubt appears in these chapters as Ma Joad questions her faith in things being so good out in California. Then Tom tells what he had heard from a California man. But they decide to live from day to day. Throughout the rest of the novel, about all they can do is to live from day to day.

Jim Casy develops more in this section. He is beginning to realize that people count more than anything else. Just being with people and hearing them laugh and talk, "all that's holy, all that's what I didn' understan'." And symbolically, as Casy is brought into the family council, it is only another step until he will be brought into the human council, that is, he is moving rapidly toward an all-encompassing view of humanity. This is again suggested when he takes over the salting of the pork, explaining that we don't have time to divide work into woman's and man's work. We must instead all help each other. This is the breaking down of traditional barriers in terms of philosophy. Ma doesn't recognize many barriers as she freely shares with all people.

Symbolically, Grampa dies in this chapter. When he refuses to leave the land, he is attempting to hold on to the last thing that he understands. After he is given the medicine and passes out, he is never fully aware of life again. Thus the removal from the land is also a death blow for him.

CHAPTER XI

Summary
When the people had left the houses vacant, then the land itself seemed more vacant, being divested of the people. Then there came the machinery and the artificial fertilizers which were not of the natural land and not of the people, and everything lost its sense of the personal.

Houses which aren't lived in cease to be houses. First animals roam in and then a wind comes in and takes off one shingle, then the next wind takes off more until soon there is nothing left.

Commentary
This intercalary chapter seems to point out part of the pathos of Grampa's situation. As Grampa is dying as a result of leaving the land, so the land which once seemed human, becomes more dehumanized. The land is now barren and vacant and mechanical and has no purpose.

CHAPTER XII

Summary
Highway 66 is the main highway from Sallisaw, Oklahoma to Bakersfield, California. It goes over mountains, then plains and more mountains and then comes to the treacherous desert. But on the other side of more mountains are the beautiful plush green valleys of California.

Onto this highway poured streams of cars which at times formed a small caravan. Along the way, they have to stop and buy parts for the cars and each person tries to cheat them. It is against the law to steal a four dollar tire, but a man can sell them a no-good tire for much more than four dollars its worth and that isn't against the law. So rather than buy from this type of man, they try to make it to the next station. Sometimes one of the people will have to walk long distances to get a spare part. But these people were in "flight from the terror behind."

Commentary

This second short intercalary chapter follows the preceding one. Usually, Steinbeck intersperses these chapters between narrative chapters. But in Chapter XI, he wanted to hint at the thematic meaning of the land being left, and in this chapter he wants the reader to get a view of the long trail and the many trials which will face the Joad family in their journey across the country.

CHAPTER XIII

Summary

As they are driving along the road, Al asks his mother if she is afraid. Ma tells him that it is just the sitting and waiting that bothers her. When there is something to do, then she will do it. About this time, Granma needs to go to the bathroom. They stop at the first clump of bushes and they decide to eat their lunch also. For the first time, they realize that they forgot to bring water along, but Al says they need gas and will stop at the next station. When they pull into the station, the attendant wants to know if they have some money. As Al starts to get angry, the man explains that many people come to him begging for a little gas. He doesn't understand. Cars are passing by every day and everyone is heading west. After some more talk, the attendant admits that he is planning on going west.

While everyone is getting a drink of water, the dog runs out in front of an oncoming car and is killed. Rose of Sharon sees it and is frightened that it will have some effect on her baby. The attendant promises to bury the dog and the Joads leave. They drive throughout the afternoon, and before dark, Ma tells Tom he had better stop because she will have to get some supper ready. Tom sees a couple parked alongside the road, and asks them if they would object to some neighbors. The couple introduce themselves as the Wilsons from up in Kansas. Their car has broken down again, and Mr. Wilson doesn't know anything about repairing cars.

As they are helping Grampa down from the truck, Noah notices that Grampa is sick. Then suddenly without warning, Grampa begins to whimper and cry. Ma tries to comfort him, and the Wilsons tell them to take Grampa inside their tent where he can lie down. Grampa tried to say something, but couldn't get the words formed. Mrs. Wilson and Casy confer and both feel that he is about to have a stroke. Granma comes in and wants to see him. She thinks that Grampa is tricky and may be sulking. Suddenly, Grampa begins to turn purple. Casy forces his mouth open and holds back the tongue. Then as Grampa breathes again, Granma starts shouting for Casy to pray, but Casy doesn't want to. But Granma is about to have a stroke also: "Pray, you, pray, I tell ya... Pray, goddamn you!" Then Casy begins to recite the Lord's prayer. While he was reciting the prayer, Grampa breathed his last breath. Mrs. Wilson takes Granma out and Casy tells Pa that it was a stroke.

The family goes into council. They decide that they will have to follow their own law and bury their own kin in spite of the fact that it is against the law. They follow the example of the earlier settlers who buried their own kin. Ma goes in to "lay out" Grampa, and Mrs. Wilson follows to help. Ma tells Mrs. Wilson that they will just use her quilt and replace it with one of their own.

When the men have dug the grave, they decide it would be best to bury a bottle with Grampa explaining who he is in case anyone ever dug him up. But they don't have pencil or paper. Mrs. Wilson fetches a pencil and tears a clear page from her family Bible. Ma wants Tom to add a word of scripture also. Mrs. Wilson tells Tom to turn to the Psalms, and there he finds something appropriate. They carry the bundle wrapped in the quilt to the grave, and Pa jumps down in order to receive the bundle in his arms. They all expect Casy to say a few words, and he talks about the living. "All that lives is holy," but now that Grampa is dead, he doesn't need much said about him.

At supper, which the two families share, the Wilsons explain that they have been on the road for three weeks, and have constantly had car trouble. Tom and Al promise to fix the car. When the subject of Grampa is brought up, Casy maintains that Grampa died when he was taken away from the farm, but just nothing could have been done about it. Al and Tom go to look at the Wilson's car, and when they come back, they suggest that the two families go together because the Joads are overloaded, and the Wilsons don't know how to keep a car running. The Wilsons are happy to accept this suggestion. Mrs. Wilson is afraid that they will be a burden, but Ma assures them that they will help each other.

Commentary

Early in the journey, Ma does not know what to do with herself. Her strength comes from facing a task and accomplishing it. It seems, too, that Ma can almost predict the future. When Al is wondering if they should have brought the preacher, Ma tells him that "You'll be glad a that preacher 'fore we're through." This later proves to be true when Casy is imposed on to bury Grampa and more important when he gives himself up to the sheriff in California so that Tom will not be suspected.

This chapter is also suggesting larger ideas concerning birth and death. First, the only dog that the Joads brought with them runs out in the road and is killed. This is the first loss of a family member or property. Then, Rose of Sharon becomes overly concerned about her baby. Even though others assure her that the sight of a dog being killed will not affect the baby, she cannot get it off her mind. The reader should remember that her baby is actually born dead, just a dried up blue mummy. But its death was from undernourishment.

More important to see is the idea of the family as a unit. The death of Grampa represents the breaking up of the smaller family unit, but at the same time, the "adoption" of the Wilsons and the Joads suggests that the individual family is being replaced by the larger concept of a world family. This is what Casy has been preaching and his words are inconspicuously being put into action.

The death of Grampa brings the Wilsons and Joads close together. We see in their actions how each is willing to help the other. This will be contrasted to the fruit growers of California who refuse to help at all and instead intentionally cheat the families by paying the smallest wages possible. Thus as soon as Grampa is dead, "the family became a unit." In deciding what to do with Grampa's body, the Joads realize the need for a special law of their own. They cannot afford to report the death, and must act as they see best. Later, in California, this idea will be developed to greater extent when the families gather together in government camps where they create and enforce their own laws.

The preacher gives a speech which would seem inappropriate at first glance for a funeral ovation. He emphasizes the living and that "all that lives is holy." Thus, we see that the emphasis is on the living, that what the living Joads are doing, even though it is against the law, is more important than a concern for the dead body. And even in the last scene where Rose of Sharon is giving life to a starving stranger, the emphasis is always on the living.

CHAPTER XIV

Summary
The great Western States do not understand the great change that is taking place in America. There is a tensing of nerves and a fear in many faces. First it was "one man, one family driven from the land." Now all through the country there are families camped alongside the road. At night one family stops by a ditch, and soon there is a small settlement. Once a man said: "I lost my land" but now he says "We lost our land."

Commentary
This very short intercalary chapter is beginning to establish a picture of the new type of society in the making. It is a migrant society, formed for a night and then broken up. And it suggests the type of action that occurred in the last chapter when the Joads pulled off the road because they saw the Wilsons already there. Furthermore, the idea of the change from *"I* lost *my* land" to *"We* lost *our* land" suggests how the individual is being submerged into a larger concept.

CHAPTER XV

Summary

All along Highway 66 there are hamburger stands and eating places. All of them have that same desperate quality of stale candy and hot coffee out of shiny pots. One waitress, Mae, saves all of her nice comments for the truck drivers. They are the ones who buy and leave a tip. Sometimes, a couple with a big rich car stop, but they make life miserable by their complaints. Instead truck drivers are pleasant and don't complain. Two truck drivers pull in and kid Mae. They order coffee and a piece of pie. Sometimes they tell a couple of jokes. While these two truck drivers are there, an old car loaded with mattresses, tents and household goods comes to a stop. They ask for some water. Then the man asks Mae to sell him a ten-cent loaf of bread. Mae tells him that she is short of bread, but offers to sell him a sandwich. The man explains that the dime must feed the entire family. Mae's husband yells to her to let the man have the bread, but he has only a dime and the bread is a fifteen-cent loaf. Again, the husband says it's alright. Meanwhile, the man's two kids are looking at the candy. The man asks if the candy is penny candy. Mae tells him it is two for a penny. The man buys two for the kids, and leaves. The truck drivers tell Mae that the candy is a nickel a piece. Mae ignores them. When the drivers leave, Mae notices that they left fifty cents each and coffee and pie cost only fifteen cents.

Commentary

This intercalary section presents part of the society touched by the new migrant society. The various stands along Highway 66 remind the reader of the plight of the "Okies," and show us how these people are viewed by others.

This chapter, however, presents its ideas through rapid, staccato scenes. And we have a broad contrast. The first narrative chapter presented the truck driver's view of a roadside restaurant, and this intercalary chapter presents the restaurant's view of the truck driver.

CHAPTER XVI

Summary

The Joads and the Wilsons continue to crawl westward. They have settled into a pattern of living. The truck leads the way and the touring car follows.

Al was driving the touring car, and Rose of Sharon was telling her mother about her and Connie's plans. They want to leave the family and move into town. At first Ma was upset, but then she realized that it was just a dream. Suddenly, Al hears some noise under the car. He blows the horn for Tom to stop. They consult and decide that it's a broken "con-rod bearing." Tom thinks it will take a day or so to get it fixed. Mr. Wilson tells them it was his fault and for the Joads to go ahead without them, but Pa refuses to do so. Tom suggests that they all get into the truck and move on because the sooner they get there, the sooner they will be earning money. He says that he and Casy will stay and get the car repaired and then will catch up with them since the car can go faster. They all consult and agree. But suddenly Ma rebels and takes out a jack handle. She tells them that she is not going and that they would have to beat her to get her to go. She tells them that the family is all they have left and she will not agree to breaking up the family. Ma is so determined in her stand that the others have to give in to her. Tom sends them on down the road to find a place for the night. He and Casy begin work on the car. Casy talks about his uneasiness, that too many people are heading West looking for work. Tom says only that he is putting one foot down at a time. He will cross that fence when he comes to it.

Later Al comes back, and they drive to the closest town in search of parts. While Al and Tom are driving there, Al tells Tom that a place for the night costs fifty cents. Al tries to get Tom to talk about the prison, but Tom tells him he would rather forget it for the present. Someday, he will tell all about it. They find a used car place with a lot of wrecked cars, and there is a car similar to theirs. The attendant is a one-eyed man who hates his boss, so he tells Tom and Al to feel free to look around. They find the piece they are looking for, and even buy a flashlight and a socket wrench for a quarter. They feel very lucky and go back and get the rod in the car that very night.

When they find the rest of the family at the camp, the proprietor tells them that they will have to pay an extra fifty cents if they want to stay. It is fifty cents a car, otherwise a deputy will arrest them for being vagrants. Tom begins to argue with the man until Pa tells Tom to stop it. Tom tells the man that he will take his car along the road a piece, but the others will stay. A man sitting on the porch asks them where they are going. Pa explains that they are heading for California in order to get work. A ragged man on the porch begins to laugh. He tells them that he has already been there and he is going back home to starve. Pa wonders about these handbills that he has seen. The man says that a rancher or landowner needs eight hundred hands and he prints five thousand handbills and then about twenty thousand people see them and come for the job. So when the workers get there, they find that there are many more people than jobs, and they have to work for wages so low that they can't earn enough to feed their families. He tells them to always find out in advance how much a person is paying in wages. It took him a long time to find out these things. In the meantime, he saw his two children die of starvation. And now his wife is also dead. Then the ragged man fades away into the darkness.

Pa is disturbed about this report, but Casy reminds them that what is true for one man is not true for another. Ma is glad to see Tom and is real anxious to get on to California "where it's rich an' green." Tom takes Uncle John and they leave for another place to stay for the night. As Tom is leaving, he throws a lump of dirt at the proprietor who had called him a bum.

Commentary
This chapter presents the further trials of the Joad family. By now, Granma is getting sicker and is almost dead. The Wilson's car breaks down, and Tom and Al must fix that. But in the same way that the Joads refuse to desert the Wilsons, Ma refuses to allow the family to separate. She makes her first strong stand in insisting that the family stay together. She knows that in their wandering all they have left is the sense of the family. "All we got is the family unbroke."

Here also we see that Casy is extending his thoughts. He is aware of the present circumstances of the people on the road. More than the others, he has noticed the changing scene. He is more aware of the large number of families traveling. And he is trying to think of the future. This contrasts with Tom who says: "I'm still layin' my dogs down one at a time."

In this chapter, the Joads run into the concept for the first time that they are vagrants and bums. This is hard for them to take, because so far they have been paying their own way, and until recently, had always thought of themselves as having land of their own.

The horrible specter of the ragged man functions like some vision of the future taken from some allegorical medieval work. His predictions for the Joads and his narration of his losses contrasts to the hopes and dreams and struggles of the Joad family.

CHAPTER XVII

Summary

Every morning, the cars of the migrant people crawled out on the highway and every night, they would huddle together. And than "a strange thing happened: the twenty families became one family." Every night then a world was established and every morning this world was torn down, and the families learned what "rights must be observed." There was the gradual establishment of rules and rights and conduct. Each night a camp would seem to have its own leaders. Seldom were there any unpleasant episodes. When a law was violated, the man was expelled from the company.

Most of the families easily adapted to this type of life. They would casually strike up relationships and would find that they knew people who came from similar parts of the country. And the first question was always: "How's the water?"

At night they talked of their homes, of their tragedies, and of the future. Sometimes someone would bring out a guitar and there would be some quiet singing. But mostly, the families needed to get rest as soon as possible so that the trip could be continued the next day.

Commentary

This is another of the intercalary chapters devoted to showing the establishment of this new migrant society. We see here that the society is building from the small family unit into the larger unit composed of about twenty families. This foreshadows the government camps that will be set up in California where the people have their own sets of laws. The emphasis is upon the fact that these people, while migrant, are not lawless people. They function best under some type of law and order, but they must be able to understand that law and order.

CHAPTER XVIII

Summary

When they reach Arizona, the Joads are stopped by a border guard who wants to know their destination and purpose. They continue slowly on their way and at last come to the border of California. They pull off on the side of the road by the side of a river. A woman scrubbing clothes warns them that a cop will be down to look them over. The Joads feel they should rest up before attempting to cross the desert. The men go down to the river, strip down and just sit in the water. Pa warns them that they only have about forty dollars left.

Soon a man and his boy show up and ask to join the Joads. They are on their way back to the Panhandle. He explains that he can't make a living in California and would rather starve with the folks he knows back home. Pa questions him about work in California. The man explains that there is lots of land that isn't being used, but it is all owned by someone who doesn't want to farm it. The people out here are scared because they know that the workers are hungry and desperate. He asks them if they have been called an "Okie" yet. He explains that an "Okie" used to mean a person from Oklahoma, but now it means a "dirty son-of-a-bitch."

Pa asks Uncle John's opinion. Uncle John says that they are going, and if they get work they will work, so they decide to try and cross the desert that night.

Tom goes over to some cool willows; Noah follows him and explains that he is not going with them. He just can't leave this nice river. He knows that his folks don't love him the way they love the other children, and he prefers to just stay by the river. Tom can't change Noah's mind, and watches him fade away down the river.

Under the spread tarpaulin, Ma is fanning Granma who seems to be out of her senses. Granma is talking at times to Grampa. Ma tries to explain to Rose of Sharon about birth and death, but soon some woman appears and wants to hold a meeting for Granma. Ma refuses, but the woman goes back to her tent and holds a meeting across the way "for a soul a 'soarin' to the Lamb." They hear the moaning and whimpering of the meeting, and after it is over, Granma seems to rest easier. They try to get some sleep, but a policeman approaches and questions Ma. He is rude and tells Ma he had better not catch them here tomorrow. "Ma's face blackened with anger," and she got a skillet and told the cop he could learn something about decency. He told Ma he didn't want any "god-damn Okies" settling down. Ma goes back under the tarpaulin, but can't understand the man's attitude.

Later, Ma tells Tom about it and he explains the words to her. He tells Ma about Noah's leaving, and Ma says nothing for a while, but then feels that the "family's fallin' apart." She reports that Granma is pretty sick, and there is not much of the salt pork left. Pa shows up and thinks that it is his fault that Noah left. They are making preparations to leave when Ivy Wilson comes and says that Sarah (Sairy) can't go. Ma wonders if they shouldn't all wait and go together, but the cop has ordered them to be gone by morning. Mr. Wilson tells them that they must leave. He asks Casy to go see Sairy. She asks Casy to pray, but Casy can't. She asks him then to just think a quiet prayer. This comforts her. She knows that she has cancer and is dying, but she doesn't want her husband to know. She feels that it will only be a few days before she is dead. As Casy leaves her, she is holding back the pain in her body.

Tom is loading the truck. They take plenty of water for the desert crossing. Pa offers Wilson two dollars and some of the pork, but he refuses to take it. Ma lays the money on the ground and the pork on top of it, and they leave.

They arrive at the desert and begin the long trip across. Connie and Rose of Sharon lie in the back and wait for everyone to get to sleep so that they can make love. Uncle John talks to Casy and asks if perhaps he is bad luck for the family because he sinned when he didn't get a doctor for his wife. And Ma is lying by Granma explaining that the family has to get across the desert. When they come to another border control station, the officer tells them that he has to inspect all of the belongings. Ma hops down and frantically tells the officers that they have an old woman who is dreadfully sick and must get to a doctor. He lets them pass. At the next town, Ma tells them that Granma doesn't need a doctor. The family is confused by Ma's actions.

After driving all night, they finally reach the mountains on the other side of the desert. Everyone gets out to look at the lovely green valleys. Ma climbs out and everyone is astonished at how sick Ma looks. She tells them that she is alright, but that Granma died early in the night. She was dead before the border control stopped them. She tells them that she explained to Granma that the family had to get across, and now Granma can lay her head to rest in the pretty green valleys of California. Everyone is awed by Ma's great strength and love.

Commentary

Arriving in California, the Joads have their first encounter with cops and first hear of the word "Okie" used in such a derogatory manner.

After the symbolic baptismal ritual in the river stream, Noah can't leave this pleasant place. Here amid the flowing waters, the Joads hear again about the drastic conditions existing in California. Noah decides that he would rather stay here than face further trials. Ma realizes that the family is breaking up. Thus, as the economic plight of the Joads becomes progressively worse, this is further symbolized by the breaking up of the family as a unit. In this chapter, Noah first leaves. Then the Joads have to part with the Wilsons, who by this time have become a part of the family. The chapter ends with the death of Granma.

Thus, as the family is breaking up, Ma's strength doubles in her attempt to hold the family together. It is almost impossible to conceive of the depth of her great strength in facing the tasks that she has to confront. Her every act is completely unselfish. She puts the welfare of the family above her personal desire. And she devotes all of her strength to holding the family together as a unit.

CHAPTER XIX

Summary
Once California belonged to Mexico, but hungry Americans came and took the land away from the complacent Mexicans. At first they only wanted to grow a little crop and were considered squatters. But gradually, these squatters grew to think that the land was theirs because they had taken their living from this land. Then they acquired more and became complacent themselves. Farming then became an industry. They imported Chinese, Japanese, Mexicans and others. They specialized in their crops. Soon, they farmed on paper only, hiring overseers to look after the land, and some of the great owners never saw their property except on paper.

Then, the great migration began. The people from Kansas, Oklahoma, and Texas began to arrive. The owners were frightened. They could not allow these hungry people to become squatters, because the squatters would begin to think of ownership. But these Okies were hungry and strong and the owners were full and soft. So the Okies settled in Hoovervilles and looked for work, and sometimes one would try to grow a secret garden in a fallow field, but a deputy would find out about it and destroy it.

The owners and the little people grew to hate these Okies. They were a threat to them. They knew that if a man and a man's children were hungry enough, that the man would do almost anything, even steal food for his starving children. So the great owners cut the wages and used the extra money to hire guards and train men to protect their property. But the Okies kept coming, and they prayed to God for a day to come when a kid can eat enough to keep from starving, and for a day to come when all the good people won't all be poor people.

Commentary

This intercalary chapter, along with Chapters XXI and XXV, is concerned with presenting the development of land ownership in California. It shows the social situation into which the migrants are trying to enter. The ownership of the land is in the hands of a few large owners. There are a few small land owners, but these are at the mercy of the large owners. Thus in a future chapter, we will see that Tom's first job—which lasted four days—was with a small owner who was told by the corporation how much he must pay in wages.

But this is not the first time this society has used migrant labor. Before the appearance of the Okies, the great owners had immigrated people from Japan, China, Mexico, etc. But the Okies presented another problem because they came from seven generations of Americans. Thus the owners cut wages in order to hire guards and policemen. But there still remained the idea that the Okies are dangerous.

The owners don't realize that the reason the Okies are dangerous is that they have such a strong faith in their people. In words that echo Carl Sandburg's poem, "We are the people," Steinbeck writes of the Okies, "Our people are good people; our people are kind people." This same idea is repeated in the next chapter by Ma Joad. She says to Tom: "Why, Tom, we're the people that live. They ain't gonna wipe us out. Why we're the people—we go on."

CHAPTER XX

Summary

Ma and Pa Joad emerge from the county coroner's office where they had to leave Granma's body. Ma is upset because Granma had set such great importance upon a proper burial. But Pa explains that it would have taken more money than they had. They drive to the edge of the town and find a camping place. It is dirty and disorderly. They drive in and begin inquiring about facilities. But the first man who meets them is incoherent. After Pa is about to explode with anger, a younger man walks over and tells them to just camp anywhere. He explains that the first man is "bull-simple," which means that too many cops have been pushing him around. Tom asks why the cops push them around and the young man explains that the people are afraid that the Okies will get organized if they stay in one place long enough. He then explains about the work situation. A man sends out handbills saying he needs so many men. Three or four times that many show up and the man cuts his wages. But there are plenty of migrants whose children haven't eaten for days and who would gladly work for a little food.

Tom wonders why the men don't get together and organize. The man explains that as soon as someone starts talking about organizing, he is arrested as a troublemaker. Tom leaves him in disgust, but the young man warns Tom that if he sees a cop, he should act bull-simple. That is the way the cops expect the Okies to act.

Tom finds Casy sitting and thinking. He is wondering how he can repay the Joads, and he is disturbed about the situation all the people are involved in. There should be a more decent life for these people, and he wonders how he can change things.

Rose of Sharon tells Connie how sick she is. Connie says that they would have been better off if they had stayed at home where he could study about tractors and get a job. Rose of Sharon reminds him that they must have a house before the baby is born. Connie walks out of the tent and down the road.

Ma is cooking a stew and the odor of it brings about fifteen kids to watch. One girl offers to keep the fire going. She wants to be invited to dinner. She tells Ma about a government camp that they once lived in. It had running water and nice toilets.

Down the line, Al talks with the same young man to whom Tom had spoken. His name is Floyd Knowles. Floyd explains that there is no work here and that men have scanned the country for any type of work. Al tells him that he will help him fix his car after supper.

Ma starts dishing up the stew. It is the first meat the family has had for days. The strange children are still standing around. Ma doesn't know what to do because she hasn't enough for her own family. After she dishes up, she leaves a little in the pot and tells the children to go get sticks and everyone can have one taste. She sets the pot down and hurries inside so that she won't have to see them. After the family eats, a woman comes to Ma and tells her that she is causing trouble by giving stew to the children. Ma explains that her family didn't have enough, but "you can't keep it when they look at you like that."

Al introduces Tom to Floyd, who tells them that there is supposed to be some work about two hundred miles north. As they are talking, a new Chevrolet comes into the camp. A man announces that he needs workers in Tulare county. Floyd asks how much he is paying. The contractor said that it depends. Floyd wants to have a contract stating how much wages they will get and then he will come. The contractor calls for the deputy, and Floyd points out that if the contractor were "on the level," he wouldn't need a deputy along. The deputy says that Floyd is the person who "busted into" a used car lot last week and arrests him. Tom speaks up for Floyd, and the deputy threatens to arrest Tom. The deputy warns the people that if they don't go to Tulare, he will have the camp burned that night. Suddenly Floyd makes a break, and as the deputy starts after him, Tom trips the deputy, who has already fired and hit one woman in the hand. Casy steps up and just as the deputy is about to fire again, he kicks the deputy in the neck. The contractor flees for help.

Casy sends Tom away, reminding him that he broke parole. When more officers arrive, Casy takes all the blame. The deputy thinks that Casy is not the right person, but they arrest him anyway.

Uncle John is dreadfully upset by this and tells the family that he has to get drunk or he will never be right again. He confesses that he held out five dollars. He takes two from Pa and gives Pa the five dollars and goes to get some whiskey. Al calls Tom out of hiding and they begin to pack up their belongings. Rose of Sharon asks after Connie. Tom tells her that he saw Connie walking off down the road. Pa maintains that Connie never was any good and it is a good riddance. Tom hears that Uncle John is off getting drunk, and he goes to find him. About a quarter of a mile down the road, he finds Uncle John lying in a ditch. Uncle John refuses to move, and Tom has to knock him out and carry him back to the camp.

As they leave the camp, they are prepared for trouble. Ma urges Tom to be careful, but he tells her that he is getting mad. The cops are "workin' on our decency." Ma reminds Tom that he has to keep clear because the "family's breakin' up." They come to a blockade where they are turned back because the deputy says: "We ain't gonna have no goddamn Okies in this town." Tom restrains himself and turns around, but he drives off the road and circles the town. Ma reminds him that they have to have patience because "us people will go on livin' when all them people is gone... We're the people that live. They ain't gonna wipe us out. Why we're the people — we go on."

Commentary

The chapter opens with the reminder of Granma's death. The Joads have had to leave her for a pauper's burial. This suggests the further disintegration of the family's standards. Previous to this, the Joads had always thought of themselves as independent. They had never asked for charity and had always paid their own way. But now this is changing rapidly.

The arrival at the first camp in California becomes a revealing event for the Joads. It is a place of extreme ugliness and contrasts to the hopes and ideals that the Joads had dreamed of when they reached California. The disorder and the filth of this place suggest again the deteriorating aspect of the Joad family. As the family is rapidly deteriorating economically and morally, the family is also breaking up as a unit in spite of everything Ma does. This chapter shows the loss of Connie and Casy, who by now must be considered a part of the family. Thus far, the family has lost its dog, Grampa, Noah, Granma, Casy, and Connie, and have had to leave the Wilsons. Thus, the family is seemingly breaking up, but it is being replaced by a larger concept. Ma expresses this at the end of the chapter when she speaks of the people. This is the concept that had earlier been advocated by Casy. The people will continue because they will help each other. As Al helps a man fix his car, so the man in turn tells Al where there might be some work. And as Ma is cooking, she cannot help but give some of her meager meal to the starving children who are looking at her. Thus, even though the immediate family does not have enough to eat, she still gives of her meager individual share to a larger family.

The Joads are also introduced or initiated into other aspects of life here in the first camp. They hear the name "Hooverville" for the first time. They learn what it means to be "bull-simple," and they hear about the cops who make people "bull-simple." They hear about the unfair working conditions and they meet, first-hand, starving children and people who have been here for a long time and can't get work.

Jim Casy's role in this chapter changes. Previously, he has been seen as a man thinking. He has been trying to solve certain dilemmas. Now he moves from thought to action. He has been searching for a way to repay the Joads and then the opportunity presents itself when Tom trips the Deputy. Casy offers himself as a sacrifice for Tom. His willingness to make the sacrifice is his method of repaying the Joads, but in a larger sense, he is now leaving the individual family in order to devote himself to the larger family of humanity. His sacrifice here and his death in a later chapter suggest that perhaps he could be viewed as a type of modern Christ-figure. His rejection of the individual family or the individual congregation in order to serve all of the people is a broad parallel to Christ's actions.

CHAPTER XXI

Summary
Suddenly, these migrant people who had lived their whole lives on forty acres now found that they have the entire West to rove around in. There were signs of panic in the West. The men of property were frightened, because they "saw the eyes of hunger." But it was good for prices. One man would work for twenty-five cents an hour and then another man would show up who would take the same job for twenty cents, and the wages went down while the prices stayed up. But the great companies did not realize that there is a thin line between hunger and anger.

Commentary

Like Chapter XIX, this intercalary chapter is showing more aspects of the idea of ownership and the California society through which the Joads are moving. It suggests that most of the little independent farmers were being caught in a trap by the larger land owning firms. But this chapter also suggests how the problem goes beyond the immediate land owners and affects the clerks in stores who are afraid for their little jobs, and these people also turn against the Okies.

CHAPTER XXII

Summary

Tom drove the family in search of the government camp, and when they arrived there was one spot which had just been vacated. Tom registers while the family unloads. He can hardly believe it when the manager tells him that there are no cops around. The people here make their own laws. He is told that a ladies' committee will call on Ma Joad tomorrow.

Early the next morning, Tom gets up and wanders around, and meets another family. He is invited to take breakfast with them. During breakfast, this family tells Tom that they have worked for twelve days and offer to take him along. They are the Wallaces. They walk to work, because earlier they had to sell their car for ten dollars. They later saw it on sale in the lot for seventy-five. Timothy Wallace explains that this job won't last but a few more days. Tom can't understand why they are cutting him in. The boss, who is somewhat sympathetic with the plight of the Okies, is being forced by the Farmer's Association to cut their wages from thirty to twenty-five cents an hour. He has no choice because his land is mortgaged and he has to obey the larger organization or he will get into trouble. He secretly tells them that there is going to be some trouble at the Saturday night dance in the government camp so that the deputies will have the right to enter and break up the camp on grounds of rioting.

Back at the camp, Ruthie and Winfield investigate the toilets, and when one flushes, they think that they have broken it. They go back and take Ma in to show her. Ma is real pleased, but a man comes in and tells her that the ladies use the other side. Ma then hears about the committee which is coming, and she bustles everyone out and tries to clean up some. While she is getting breakfast, the manager comes by. At first Ma is suspicious, but then she realizes that she is back among her own type of people. Rose of Sharon comes back and tells of the shower stalls and that she has already taken a shower. Ma is real happy, and goes to take one also. While she is gone, some woman (a religious fanatic) comes by and frightens Rose of Sharon by telling her how sinful people here are and how she knows people whose baby was born black and dead because of their sins. Ma returns and reassures Rose of Sharon that it is all nonsense.

The committee appears and Ma and Rose of Sharon go with the members to learn all about the camp. She hears how the camp has a small amount of credit at a store for people who are really destitute. She hears many other stories about the camp from the members of the committee.

Meanwhile, Pa, Uncle John, and Al are out looking for work. Everywhere they look there are signs already which say "No Help Wanted: No Trespassing." They pick up another man from the camp who tells them that he has searched for work all week and can't find any. They decided to head back to camp and save gasoline.

After the committee left, Ma is making plans when Rose of Sharon sees the lady who frightened her coming toward the tent. The lady introduces herself as Mrs. Sandry. She begins talking about how wicked the people in the camp are. Ma disagrees with her, but Mrs. Sandry insists on running down everyone as evil. Ma picks up a stick of wood and tells her to get away. At that moment, Mrs. Sandry "threw back her head and howled. Her eyes rolled up, her shoulders and arms flopped loosely." Some men had to pick her up and carry her back to her own tent. The manager explains to Ma that the woman is mentally sick, and is always causing trouble. When Pa and Uncle John get back, Ma has everything under control, but tells Pa that she spends her time thinking about things that bother her. Pa is depressed since he couldn't find work, but Ma tells him that he didn't look everywhere and something will turn up later. She is optimistic because Tom got work that very morning.

Commentary

This chapter functions as a contrast to the preceding one. The contrast is seen in a comparison of the types of camps and the reception in each camp. Whereas they were met at Hooverville by a "bull-simple" migrant, here they are cordially received by the manager. In Hooverville, there was disorder and filth. Here order and cleanliness prevail. The fear of the cops at Hooverville is replaced by confidence in the committee which rules the camp. Therefore, by contrast, this government camp seems to be a real paradise.

The fact that there are no cops is a salvation for Tom. He was to the point of explosion if he had to face another cop, and his stay here gives him time enough to recover somewhat, and here he finds the friendliness that he needed. The way he is received and offered some breakfast is reassuring. Ma is also reassured by the people in the camp. She feels that she is now back with her own kind of people.

Other than sharing breakfast with Tom, these new people also share their work, even though they know it won't last very long. Thus, we see that it is not just Ma Joad who is willing to share. It is a common trait among these people.

The manner in which Tom takes to his work shows that he is not just a drifter. He could easily become a meaningful member of society if he were given a chance.

The cleanliness, the reception, and the friendliness of the government camp plus the fact that Tom has some work almost blinds the reader to the real situation. This promise of hope, of something better, only makes the forthcoming trials more bitter. Furthermore, we must remember that however much better this place is than was Hooverville, the Joads are still living a migratory existence. This is not the little white house that Ma Joad dreamed of. In other words, the goodness of this place is not in itself but only in comparison to the Hoovervilles which are so much worse.

CHAPTER XXIII

Summary

The migrant people search for work, but in between the frantic efforts to live, they create pleasure. Some gather together at night and narrate tales of earlier lives, or some relate episodes involving ancestors. Some "spoke in great rhythms, others spoke in great words because the tales were great." And if the person had any money, he could get drunk, and then the loneliness and frustration faded away for a brief time. Then he could feel "that everything's holy—everything, even me."

Sometimes a person would bring out a harmonica. This instrument is easy to carry. Another would produce a guitar while still another brings a fiddle. The three could then create a little pleasant music, playing the old-fashioned songs that everyone knew.

In another place a preacher would preach about evil and lead people through agonies of salvation until the people groveled and whined on the ground.

Commentary

This is another intercalary chapter devoted to showing the migrant society. Here Steinbeck is implying that these are the type of people from which great folk epics and folk music are created. There is the sense of something mythic about these tales, and the way that the people get together and create music. Steinbeck offers one tale that has a certain folk and mythic quality, and the reader can easily imagine another person taking the same tale and narrating it again and adding his own touch until the tale becomes a part of the culture.

CHAPTER XXIV

Summary

On Saturday, the government camp begins its bathing early in the afternoon in preparation for the dance that night. Ezra Huston, chairman of the central committee, reports his progress. He has added twenty extra people to his committee. These people are to dance and move in on any trouble and quietly stop it. They have been instructed not to hurt anyone. None of them can understand why the Land Owners want to destroy the camp.

Rose of Sharon doesn't want to go to the dance because of her condition. She is still worrying about Connie. Willie Eaton comes and tells Tom that he is to be on the front gate with an Indian named Jule. He is to check the guests and make sure no troublemakers get in. He leaves with Willie, and Ma comforts Rose of Sharon telling her that they will go hear the music and if anyone wants to dance with Rose of Sharon, Ma will explain that she is sick.

At the gate, Jule immediately spots three guys who say that a Mr. Jackson invited them. Jule tells Tom to follow them and get in touch with Jackson. When they find Jackson, he said that he once worked with these guys, but didn't invite them. Now the committee feels that it has the right guys spotted, but will leave them alone unless they start trouble.

The dance begins and everything goes smoothly for a while. Then one of the three goes over and insists upon dancing with another's girl. Immediately the committee spots them and moves in. The three are quietly apprehended, but in the first confusion, someone blew a whistle.

Immediately, a carload of deputies drove to the gate, demanding that the guard open up because they hear there is a riot inside. The guard tells them to listen to the quiet music. The deputies pull back and wait.

The three men are carried to Mr. Huston. He questions them and notices that they are migrants themselves. He doesn't understand why the men want to turn against their own people. He instructs the men to put these three over the back fence without hurting them. But he warns them that next time he won't let them off so easily.

Later that night, one migrant tells how in Akron once the mountain people were hired as cheap labor and then joined the union. The people in the town started buying arms and gasoline. The mountain people called for a "Turkey Shoot." All they did was to walk five thousand strong through the town each carrying a rifle. Since then, the town people have left them alone. The migrant man thinks that perhaps they should have a Turkey Shoot.

Commentary

This shows the effect of good organization. In showing the way the migrants can work together to achieve their goals, this chapter implies that these people have the ability to work well and efficiently given the opportunity. The ease with which they solve a difficult problem and save their camp suggests the advantage of organizing.

Thus when the men talk about why the Land Owners want to destroy the camp, we see here the exact reason. With a little effort, these people could organize all over California. The Owners know this and destroy the camps to prevent this organization.

This chapter is especially poignant in the way that the committee insists on no violence and no brutality. In view of all the brutality the migrants have had to suffer, this action offers itself as far more humane than the actions of the more educated Land Owners.

The final part of the chapter, when the man narrates the story of the Turkey Shoot, prepares us for some attempt at organization by the men in a subsequent chapter.

CHAPTER XXV

Summary

"The spring is beautiful in California." There are fruit blossoms covering every hillside. Valleys are long miles of green vegetables just beginning to grow. They are the result of years of experimentation by scientists hired by the land owning firms. The small owner has benefited by these experiments also. But since he must sell his fruit and produce to the larger canneries which are owned by the same land owning firms, he cannot afford to gather his harvest. The large firms have built their own canneries and they sell their own farm products to their own canneries at a very cheap rate. Then they make their money on the canned produce which is kept at the same price. So the small owner has to sell his produce at such a low price to the large land owner's cannery that he can't pay to have his fruit picked and harvested. Thus more and more of the small farms are becoming the property of the large land owning firms.

In the souls of people, many people, "The grapes of wrath are filling and growing heavy, growing heavy for the vintage."

Commentary

Steinbeck showed in an earlier narrative chapter how one small farmer was at the mercy of the larger firms. Now he offers a generalized view of these smaller farmers being squeezed out by underhanded tactics of the larger firms. That is, the larger firms force wages down and keep the prices so low, but at the same time keep the price of the canned product high, and in this way they are forcing the small owner to sell out to the larger owner. Soon many of these small farmers will be migrants like the Okies.

CHAPTER XXVI

Summary

Some time later, Ma stops all the men and tells them that they must have a meeting and decide something. She points out she has only enough flour and lard for two more days and only ten more potatoes left, and they haven't had any work with the exception of the four days work that Tom had. Pa hates to leave because it is so nice in the camps. But Ma says that they can't eat niceness. Everyone is glad that Ma brought the subject out in the open, but they don't know what to do about it. It is finally decided that they will have to leave in the morning. They don't have enough gas to go far, but they must make an effort. Everyone splits up to make preparations. Ma tries to comfort Rose of Sharon who believes that her baby will be born deformed. Ma cheers her up by giving her some gold earrings and then piercing her ears.

Al strolls down and finds a girl he has been sleeping with. He promises her that he will make some money and then come back. Pa saw some fellows and told them he was leaving even though he hated to do so. Tom joined some of his friends and they talk about all the people getting together and organizing.

It is still dark when Ma gets everyone up. She gives them some cold biscuits to eat, and they check out of the camp. They notice that winter is coming, and Ma tells Tom that they must have some type of house before winter, because little Winfield is not strong. Ma says that she is losing her "spunk" especially at night time when she has to think about the family's condition.

The truck has a flat and while they are fixing it, a man comes by and tells them where there is work. It is only thirty-five miles away, and they head that way immediately, hoping to get some work that very day. They talk about what they will buy with money earned the first day.

When they arrive at the town, they are met by many cops, and told that the wages are five cents a box. They are led through a throng of people who are shouting things. The people look like Okies and migrants. Tom asks what the trouble is, and a patrolman tells him to mind his own business. They are let inside a huge fence and told to unload in shack number sixty-three. The men unload and head immediately for the peach orchard.

Tom hurriedly picks a box of peaches and takes it in for credit, but the manager tells him that the peaches are bruised and unacceptable. He has to start over, and he tells the others to start over. It takes much longer this way. Ruthie and Winfield come out and Pa tells them that they must work. He has them pack the peaches gently in a box. Later Ma comes out, and with all seven working, they have earned a dollar by night. Ma goes with a credit slip to the store where she finds that the prices are higher here than in town, and also of an inferior quality, but she can do nothing about it. She spends her dollar and still doesn't have enough to feed the family. She asks for a little sugar on credit since the men are still picking peaches. But the man cannot allow it. Ma pleads with the clerk and he finally pays for the sugar himself, and gives it to Ma. Ma thanks him and says "If you're in trouble or hurt or need – go to poor people. They're the only ones that'll help –."

At supper, Ma serves all that she was able to buy, and says that they made a dollar and ate a dollar's worth and they are still hungry. Tom says he is going to see what the trouble was outside the fence. But Pa wants to stay and Al goes looking for a girl. Tom heads for the gate, but the guard won't let him out. He goes back and climbs under a fence. At the first tent, he meets Jim Casy. Jim tells him about his experiences in jail, especially when all the prisoners were served some sour beans. All started yelling at the same time and they were given something better to eat. Now Casy is trying to organize the people. He and the people on the outside had come to the orchard to pick for five cents a box, but the owners cut it to two and a half cents a box. The men went on strike. Since then they have been driven like pigs.

Tom tells Casy about the law and order in the government camp. Casy wants it to be this way all over. He knows that tomorrow, the price will be cut back to two and a half cents a box even though the Joads got five cents today.

Suddenly they hear men approaching. They try to get away, but Jim and Tom are stopped. Casy tells them: "you don't know what you're doin'. You're helpin' to starve kids." But just as he said it, a man hit him with a pick handle and crushed his head. Tom became enraged, grabbed the pick handle and crushed the cop's head. Another man struck Tom in the head, but he was able to get away. He hid in some brush, and gradually worked his way back to the camp.

The next morning, his face is swollen and bloody. His nose is broken, and he tells his folks that he must leave. Ma will not allow this. She says that he needs protection and hiding, and the members of the family are the only people he can trust. They go out to pick enough to get gas to leave. That night they make a cave out of mattresses and hide Tom in there and drive out of the camp. Down the road, Tom notices a sign asking for cotton pickers. He tells his folks that he will hide in the nearby creek. They agree, and Tom takes a blanket with him and goes into hiding.

Commentary

This chapter opens with Ma forcing the men to perform some action. She is the moving force behind the family. It seems as though the menfolk have refused to face up to the situation, and have done nothing. Thus, in this chapter, Ma begins to assume the leadership. At the same time, she knows that this is dangerous, because the men can be completely defeated when a woman assumes command. She knows how far to go. As she tells Tom: "Take a man, he can get worried, an' worried, an' it eats out his liver, an purty soon he'll jus' lay down and die with his heart et out. But if you can take an' make 'im mad, why, he'll be awright." This is what she has done for Pa Joad. And later after they have picked peaches for a half a day, Pa seems relieved to work and not have to think any more: "seems like I jus' been beatin' my brains to death for a hell of a long time. I'm gonna set awhile, an' then go to bed."

But after Tom has killed the man, it is again up to Ma to act. She knows that Pa is incapable of facing such a large decision. She tells Tom: "Pa's lost his place. He ain't the head no more...There ain't no fambly now." Thus, Ma feels that she has to take control. It is, then, Ma who decides that they must leave the camp and hide Tom. Even Pa recognizes his decline when he tells Tom "Seems like the man ain't got no say no more." But the reader must remember that Ma's assumption of leadership is done so as to hold the family together. She would most willingly relinquish leadership as soon as there is food and shelter and security.

As the Joads are being pushed about more and more, there is an emphasis on the meanness of people. Everyone is getting mean. The cops are getting harsher, and even the pickers get into mean arguments about who has the right to pick at a tree. Ma comments that even the jokes that are told are mean jokes. There is no happiness and no pleasure in anything any more. When the cops attack Casy so fiercely and murder him, Tom's repressed meanness is released. Thus, this scene parallels Tom's predicament some four years ago when he killed his first man.

But Tom is beginning to broaden his view of life. Previously, he was concerned only for his own pleasure. Then he has devoted himself to the family's benefit. Now Tom is becoming involved in a larger humanity. He tries to involve Pa Joad and Al, but none of them is interested. Thus, Tom goes alone to investigate the crowd and noise they observed on the way into the camp. His concern leads him into Jim Casy.

Casy is now emerging as a Christ figure. Earlier he had gone into the wilderness in order to figure things out. Now he has been in jail and seen how organizations can be effective. He has heard of the good law and order in the government camps. Thus, he is trying to organize the people and has led them on a strike for better wages. But there are now more people, like the Joads, who have come in. Jim tries to get Tom to be his emissary (or disciple) and go back into the camp and explain the situation to the people inside, but Tom is not yet ready to assume full responsibility for these types of acts. He says he will try, but he has no hopes of success. As soon as Casy is killed, Tom must revenge his death. Note also that Casy dies as did Christ, saying "You don't know what you're a-doin'." It will require more thinking on Tom's part before he is ready to take up and complete Casy's mission.

As they are escaping from the camp, a small cave is made out of mattresses for Tom to hide in. There is a bit of irony here, since in the first chapters, Tom refused to sleep in the cave that Muley Graves showed him. Then he sees the culvert where he will hide until his wounds heal. Ironically, these are also freudian womb images, used to suggest obversely that Tom is slowly being prepared to separate from his family. In other words, it is a return-to-the-womb in preparation for a rebirth.

CHAPTER XXVII

Summary
There were now signs appearing advertising for cotton pickers, and those who didn't have cotton sacks could buy one and the fee would be taken out of the first hundred and fifty pounds picked. And

the wages weren't bad. Eighty cents a hundred for the first time over and ninety cents the second time over. But there were so many pickers that there was a story of a man who never got his cotton sack paid for. Sometimes the scales were fixed, and sometimes they weren't. The people never knew. But at the end of every day of picking, there would be some meat for supper.

Commentary

This chapter prepares us for the Joad's experiences with picking cotton. The Joads, as the other migrants, are hoping the cotton will last as the cotton picking episode is a short respite from hunger, but it will be the last work that the Joads will get.

CHAPTER XXVIII

Summary

The Joads are one of the first families to reach the cotton fields and therefore get one of the boxcars to live in. They must, however, share the boxcar with another family. They made enough to buy new overalls and a new dress for Ma, and they had meat every night. But one night Ma let Winfield and Ruthie have a box of Cracker Jacks. Suddenly Winfield comes in and tells Ma that Ruthie has told about Tom's hiding out. He explains that Ruthie got beaten up by a big girl because she was bragging about her Cracker Jacks. Ruthie threatened the big girl and told about her brother who had killed two men and was hiding.

Ma feels that she must go immediately to Tom. She puts two pork chops and some potatoes on a plate and heads for where Tom is hiding. She has to wait some time. When he comes, he leads her back to his cave. Ma tells him about Ruthie. Then she tells him that he must go. She asks him to come closer so she can touch him because she can't see him. "I wanta remember, even if it's on'y my fingers that remember." Tom tells her about his thinking, about how Casy told him about the one big soul and we are just pieces of that big soul. "His little piece of a soul wasn't so good 'less it was with the rest, an' was whole." So Tom explains that he has to finish the work that Casy started. He is going out and see if he can organize the people. Ma reminds him that they killed Casy, but Tom assures her that he will duck faster. She makes him take some money she has saved and they part.

On the way back home, a small farmer tells Ma that he needs pickers tomorrow. He has only twenty acres. When she gets back to the car, Mr. and Mrs. Wainwright, the family who share the other end of the boxcar, tell the Joads that they are worried because Al is going out every night with their sixteen-year old Agnes. Ma and Pa promise to talk to Al. After they are gone, Pa tells Ma that it looks as though their life is about over, but Ma refuses to believe such talk.

Al comes in and tells his folks that he and Agnes are going to get married. The Joads are glad and they join with the Wainwrights and make some pancakes to celebrate. They tell the Wainwrights about the cotton picking and they decide to all go together. Early next morning, they start out for the field. But so many people show up for the twenty acres that it is all picked out by eleven o'clock. Rose of Sharon had gone along, and on the way back it began to rain. By the time they reached the boxcar, the rain was pouring down, and Rose of Sharon was having chills.

Commentary

In spite of the fact that Tom is forced to hide out, this chapter presents a brief respite in the Joad decline. They are able to work and eat. But there are suggestions and hints of the forthcoming despair. It is fall weather now. The Joads have no money and no job, and at the end of the chapter, it is beginning to rain.

In spite of the brief respite, in the larger view of the novel, the Joad family continues to decline. In this chapter, we leave Tom, thus diminishing the family once more. Furthermore, Al announces his intention to marry Agnes and he will soon be lost to the family.

When Ma goes to the cave where Tom is hiding, the images suggest a "return-to-the-womb." There is the brush and the long passageway and the darkness, and Ma must feel Tom to make sure he is there. But as suggested in the last chapter, this "return-to-the-womb" image is used to suggest Tom's rebirth. Earlier he was interested in only himself. Then he devoted himself to the family. Now he tells Ma that he must go out and help all of humanity. His wounded nose suggests that he is now changed physically, and he also changes mentally. When he emerges this time, there is the suggestion that he will become the great leader and organizer for these migrant people. He will become the disciple who will carry on Casy's work. And where Casy was too idealistic (he talked too much) to put his plan into action or whereas he was the Christ figure, it will be Tom who will formulate and activate Casy's idealism. The images should not be carried too far, but the reader should be aware of a slight correlation between Christ and Paul and Casy and Tom. And Tom realizes the importance of Casy's message only after Casy died for these ideas.

When Ma was planning the trip West during the first chapters of the novel, she was worrying about the future. Tom advised her to face only one day at a time. Now Ma has learned Tom's lesson and says to Pa and Uncle John "Jus' live the day." And she reassures the family that "We ain't gonna die out. People is goin' on—changin a little, maybe, but goin' right on."

Pa, however, feels his defeat. He even admits to Tom that "Ma is taken' over the fambly. Woman sayin' we'll do this here an' we'll go there. An' I don' even care."

CHAPTER XXIX

Summary

Over the coast mountains, grey rain clouds were beginning to form. Then the rain began, slowly at first, but continued. A few puddles formed in low places, then little ponds, and finally lakes. The streams and rivers worked themselves up to overflowing. Tents, old cars were drowned out and people were engulfed in mud. If a barn was to be found on a high place, it was crowded with people existing in hopeless despair. Then the men and boys went out to beg for food, even rotten vegetables from store owners. Then they would steal. They would go to a chicken house and take a chicken and would not bother to run if the owner shot at them. And the women watched the men to see if "the break had come at last." But they saw that fear was turning to anger and all was alright and "the break would never come as long as fear could turn to wrath."

Commentary

This is the last intercalary chapter and predicts the rains that will drown out the Joads in the next chapter. It gives us an intimation of what will happen to the Joads after the formal close of the novel.

As the first intercalary chapters worked around the idea that the "women and children knew deep in themselves that no misfortune was too great to bear if their men were whole," so then, the last chapter closes with the women still watching their husbands to see if the break has yet come.

CHAPTER XXX

Summary

On the second day of the rains, Al took the tarpaulin down and covered the motor of the car. Then the Wainwrights and the Joads became one family. They wonder if they shouldn't leave, but at least the boxcar is dry. Rose of Sharon is down with a cold and high fever. Pa decides to try to build a bank to keep the water away. He goes to see if the other men will help.

Rose of Sharon's fever brings on labor pains. When Pa comes back and finds Rose of Sharon in labor, he tells the men that they must build the embankment because his girl is having a baby. The men work frantically trying to build a dam faster than the water is rising. They work well into the night, piling more and more mud on top of branches used to solidify the dam. They are succeeding in blocking out the water, but suddenly, a tree is washed into the embankment and knocks a huge hole in it allowing the water to gush out and flood the entire place. Al runs immediately and tries to start the old truck, but the battery won't start it. By the time he got the crank out, the truck was too deeply submerged in water and had to be abandoned.

When Pa returns to the boxcar, he is shown a "blue shriveled little mummy" which never had a chance to live. He asks Ma what he should have done. He wonders if he couldn't have done something. Pa goes out to talk to the men, and Mrs. Wainwright comes down so Ma can get some rest. They talk about helping each other and Ma says "Use' ta be the fambly was fust. It ain't so now. It's anybody. Worse off we get, the more we got to do."

Pa and Al and Uncle John take a sight on the rising water to see if it will come into the box car. They think it will not completely flood the place but will cover the floor of the boxcar before it overflows the highway embankment. They decide to take part of the truck bed and build a platform in the boxcar to keep their things dry. Mrs. Wainwright asks one of the men to take the dead baby and bury it. This is against the law, but they can't help it. Uncle John takes the box with the baby in it and goes out with a shovel. But instead of burying it, he places it in the stream where it floats away.

Pa goes to the store to get something for breakfast. When he returns with some bread and bacon, Ma asks him if they have any more money left. Pa tells her he spent it all. They build the platform and place their stuff on it. When the flood comes into the boxcar, they all huddle together on the platform. On the second day, Pa went out and came back with ten potatoes. The family ate these and stayed another night. The next morning, Ma decided it was time to go. Al says that he will stay with Agnes and Ma tells him to watch their stuff and they will come back as soon as possible. Pa carries Rose of Sharon on his back, and Ma carries Winfield, and Uncle John carries Ruthie. As they hurry out, Pa asks where they are hurrying to. Ma sees a barn that looks dry. They cut across a field to reach it.

They find some dry hay in the barn, and suddenly they saw a man lying on his back with a boy huddling close to him. The boy explains that his father is starving: "He ain't et for six days." The boy stole some bread, but the man vomited it up. He needs soup or milk. Ma tells him not to worry, and asks for the boy's dry blanket for Rose of Sharon. She gets the wet clothes off Rose of Sharon and looks askingly to Rose of Sharon who understands what Ma wants and nods in agreement. Ma wraps Rose of Sharon in the blanket and leads the others out of the barn. Rose of Sharon goes to the man and lies down by him. She gently takes his head and leads it to her full breasts.

Commentary

Rose of Sharon had dreamed of having her own place when the baby was born and of having a doctor. But the conditions under which she actually gives birth to the baby serve to destroy all of her dreams. She will now be a changed person. She feels the next day the surging milk in her breasts and realizes for the first time the full meaning of her womanhood.

When it is known that Rose of Sharon is in labor, Pa rises to his one last great effort. He organizes the men to help build the dam and to keep the water away from their camp. It looks as though he will succeed in his efforts until suddenly a fallen tree destroys all the efforts. With this failure, Pa relinquishes all efforts to run the family. He turns pleadingly to Ma for help, understanding, and instructions. When Ma says it is time to leave the boxcar, Pa can do nothing but obey.

For all of Ma's efforts to hold the family together, it continues to disintegrate. Now Al is separated from the family, but at the same time, Ma now realizes that there is something greater than the family. She now comes around to Casy's (and later Tom's) views. She says to Mrs. Wainwright that the family used to be first, but now it is anyone who needs help. Ma has become then a part of a greater human society than is represented solely by the family.

With the close of the novel, the Joads' plight is at its lowest ebb. They have no money, they have abandoned their car and property, they have no food, they are wet and sickly, and they have to face the oncoming winter with no place to live and no work. But in spite of these distressing things, the novel ends on an affirmative note. Rose of Sharon is giving life to a dying stranger. There is the realization of the need of each individual to help another regardless of who he is.

GENERAL MEANING

Essentially, *The Grapes of Wrath* is a plea for the land own-ers of California to be more tolerant. The novel is told from the viewpoint of a migrant family, the Joads, who are forced off their land in Oklahoma and who seek employment in California.

During the course of the novel, the Joads move from a concern only for themselves and their own personal welfare to a concern for all the people of the world. Early in the novel, we meet an itiner-ant preacher who has been drifting for four years and has arrived at an Emersonian view of the world. He believes that all the people are holy and that his soul is only a little piece of a larger soul. He is unable to do anything about his views until he reaches California. Here he sacrifices himself for another man (Tom Joad) and goes to jail. In jail he learns the value of the small people organizing. He tries to lead the people on a strike and is killed brutally by some cop in California, but he has had an influence on the Joads.

It is Tom Joad, a man who has been in prison, that Casy most influences. Early in the novel, Tom Joad was concerned only for himself. Then he moved toward a concern for the family, and at the end of the novel, he is going out to see if he can organize the Okies (migrants) even though he knows this involves him in great per-sonal danger.

The same concern for humanity at large is seen in Ma Joad. At first she was concerned with keeping the family together. But as the novel progresses she begins to become a part of a larger human family. As she says in the end of the novel, at first it was the family and now it is just anyone who needs help.

Thus with the Joads, the journey West is also a journey from the personal concern to a larger concern for all of humanity. This change is accompanied by a change also in the Joad's economic situ-ation. As the Joads deteriorate economically, they seem to enlarge their view of humanity. At the first camp in California, they don't have enough to feed their own family, but Ma leaves a little some-thing in the bottom of the pot for some strange children, who have been standing around. Therefore, in the largest view, the decline of the family and the decline of the economic situation are accompanied by an increase in and acceptance of a larger view of humanity.

STYLE

During the narrative parts of the novel, Steinbeck keeps his style as simple as possible. He is anxious to capture the very basic elements of the story. He uses dialect in his characters' speeches to capture the realistic nature of their speech. And the emphasis of the story is on the narrative element. Consequently, he maintains as much as possible a straightforward narrative style.

During the intercalary chapters, he varies his style considerably. In the chapter on the turtle, (Chapter III), he used a symbolic approach combined with realistic description. In the chapter on Highway 66, he uses a staccato style which makes the reader feel the beeping of the autos and the speeding of the cars as we stand along the road and watch them rush by. Some of the chapters are almost poetic in their style. Mr. Peter Lisca in his book *The Wide World of John Steinbeck* suggests that some of the chapters could be broken down into poetry similar to the poetry found in the "Bates Bible."

Other of these intercalary chapters are written as essays or as historical accounts of past events. Some are offered by the author himself, but they all vary according to the purpose intended by the subject matter.

CHARACTER ANALYSIS

Ma Joad

Ma Joad is the strength of the family. She was strong and enduring. Her face showed that it was controlled and kindly. Ma has spent her life controlling and gauging her emotions for her family's benefit. Her eyes showed that she had experienced almost everything, and has passed beyond suffering and pain to become inpenetrable. She was always expected to be calm and allow nothing to disturb her. Her understanding was acknowledged by the rest of the family to be supreme. "Since old Tom and the children could not know hurt or fear unless she acknowledged hurt and fear, she had practiced denying them in herself." But her greatest attribute was her calmness. She was imperturbable in all things. Her position in the family demanded that her hands be those of the healer, the comforter, the authority. And from her position in the family, she had achieved a sense of quiet dignity and a "clean calm beauty."

Ma knew that if she ever showed fear or despair, that if she ever fluctuated away from perfect control, the entire family would collapse. Therefore, she maintained a front before the family that never faltered.

She functions in the novel as the living embodiment of the thoughts of Jim Casy. Casy believes that all is holy and every action is a holy action. He also maintains that all of God's creatures deserve a little goodness and a chance to live a decent life. In Ma Joad's every action, there is concern for her own family and when the occasion arises, she extends herself to help other people. She is a great comfort to the Wilsons and forces them to accept money and food when they are parting. She feeds the starving faces of the unknown children when she barely has enough for her own family, and she is the comfort and judge in her relations with the Wainwrights.

Ma Joad is the force which holds the family together. She realizes now that they have no home and that the only value and meaning in life is that which they derive from being a family. In spite of this, she knows that the family is breaking up. But she fights against it in every way possible. She keeps the two cars together so the family won't be separated and she forces decisions to be made for the benefit of the family.

Ma Joad understands the inner need of each individual member of the family. She knows that if Pa is ever defeated completely, the family will collapse. So at times, she intentionally goads Pa into anger, and he will come back disgusted but filled with more energy. She knows how Rose of Sharon is troubled by her pregnancy. She knows the quiet strength in Tom. And she knows that Al does not possess the sense of responsibility that Tom has. She understands Uncle John's need to get drunk and does not criticize him for it. Thus as long as the family or some part of the family is together, Ma will see to it that they keep going. Because she feels and knows that they are the people, that they are the ones who will endure and continue to live and populate the world, she expresses the great maxim of the novel, that is, when a man is in trouble, go to poor people, they are the only ones who will help.

Pa Joad

Pa is not so distinctly characterized as is Ma Joad. Essentially, he is a hard-working tenant farmer who does not quite understand what happened. He attempted to farm in the same way that his fore-fathers had farmed, and every year it became necessary to borrow a little more from the bank until one day the farm was no longer his. Then he became a migrant. He still didn't understand what happened.

He is not a man who is afraid of work. He is not depicted as a lazy mirgrant or as a lazy farmer. He was a victim of forces he could not understand and forces against which he could not compete.

Pa is the titular head of the family. His view of the family is more narrow than is Ma's. Whereas Ma is quite willing to take the preacher Jim Casy along with them, it is only Pa who wonders if they have enough for an extra mouth. But this is not a selfish concern. He is responsible for feeding the family, and he feels this responsibility. He is devoted to Ma, respects her and even though he is expected to make the decisions, he looks to Ma for guidance and strength.

Pa's supreme original effort in the novel is a failure. When the flood comes, he recruits help and tries to build a small dam to keep the water out. He works fiercely and diligently, but is unable to stop the encroaching flood waters. Thus, at the end of the novel, the man who earlier resented Ma's control and bossing, looks to Ma for instructions and when Ma says they have to leave, he puts Rose of Sharon on his back and they leave. Thus, at the end, Pa is closer to defeat than is Ma Joad, and he must in the future take his strength from her.

Grampa and Granma

They are a delightfully depicted couple. They seem to thrive on quarreling and fighting and competing. There is obviously a strong attraction between them, but neither would admit it. Instead, they delight in annoying each other. Grampa is anti-religious so Granma becomes devotedly religious. She is said to have had some howling trances where she could whine and moan with the best of the fanatics. Once, Grampa tried to boss Granma, and she took it so long and then got a shotgun and shot his buttocks full of buckshot. Since that day, he has respected her more.

Since Granma is religious, Grampa delights in being as vulgar as possible. He uses the worst language, and at his advance age still likes to talk about his escapades. But Granma's religion is an unusual one. At times we think it is only to annoy Grampa. The phrase that best characterizes her religion occurs when the preacher Casy won't pray, and she says to him: "Pray goddamn you, pray."

Grampa belonged to the land. Thus as soon as he was removed from the land, he died. And Granma seemed to take her strength from arguing and competing with Grampa; thus, she does not live long after Grampa's death.

Uncle John

Long ago, Uncle John was married to a young girl to whom he was rather devoted. She was in her fourth month of pregnancy when she developed severe pains in her stomach. She asked Uncle John to get a doctor, but he told her that she had "et too much." By the next day, the woman was out of her head, and in the afternoon she was dead. Uncle John has never recovered from this experience. He goes through spells when he must get completely drunk in order to face life. Sometimes he will search out women to sleep with. But essentially, he lives a quiet life and disturbs no one. His guilt feelings force him into the background, but whenever he is around children, he is always slipping them gum or some other trinket.

When Uncle John is not in one of his spells of drinking or fornicating, he moves quietly and unobserved. He seldom speaks in the novel, and when there is work to be done, he works constantly, never varying his speed.

Tom Joad

In some ways, Tom Joad is the main protagonist. The novel opens with his hitchhiking home from the state prison at McAlester. We find out that four years ago, he got in a fight with a man who knifed him. Trying to protect himself, he hit the man with a shovel and killed him.

When Tom emerges from the prison, we see that he is interested only in his own personal comforts and wants. As he tells Jim Casy, "I'm just gonna lay one foot down before another." He feels no guilt or shame about having killed a man and under the same circumstances would do it again. He does not regret that the man is dead, but Tom feels he was only defending himself.

After four years in prison, Tom is anxious to taste all the comforts of life. When he finds his people gone and then meets Muley Graves, he is disappointed. He refuses to sleep in the cave and hide from cops on his own land. Later, as fortune turns against Tom and the Joad family, he must take refuge in a cave after he has killed the cop in California.

Essentially, Tom is a rather steady person who does not like to be pushed around. He values his individuality and his independence. Thus, when the cops begin pushing him around, he has to find something like the government camp so as to regain his strength. He previously assured Ma Joad that he was not "mean-mad" like Purty Boy Floyd, but the more the cops push him around, the more Tom turns towards violence.

Earlier he had listened only half-heartedly to the words that Jim Casy preached. But after he has endured foul treatment, mortification and shame at the hands of the land owners and the California cops, he begins to reconsider Jim Casy's words. After Jim's death and after Tom has had to hide in the cave and brush, he has time to think over the things that Casy has said. He knows now that man cannot live alone, that man must join together with other men because strength comes from unity. Thus, during the course of the novel, Tom moves from a strictly independent way of thinking only of his own comfort to a devotion to the family and an attempt to help the family at the expense of his own personal comfort. His final statement is that he must now move away from the family, and accept all the world as his family. He is now going forth to carry on the work begun by Jim Casy. When Ma warns Tom that they killed Casy, he tells her that Casy didn't duck soon enough. Casy was perhaps too much a talker and too much an idealist. It will be left for Tom to carry out in practical ways the theoretical aspects of Jim Casy's philosophy.

Rose of Sharon

As her name implies, Rose of Sharon is searching for romance and beauty in life. She is, most of the time, sick and whining, especially after Connie leaves her. One could contribute it to her pregnancy, but she seems exceptionally petulant. Her tendency to credit every event as having an effect upon the baby becomes overbearing after a while. Of course, her baby was just a little blue mummy, but it was the result of undernourishment and not of spells and bad events that she saw. But she comes into her own after she has suffered the pains and pangs of childbirth. It is as though having delivered herself of a baby, she now assumes a fullness of life to equate with the fullness of her breasts. Thus the novel closes on Rose of Sharon's giving life to some unknown starving man. This is her first action, which extends beyond a concern for herself. She is now a part of that brotherhood of man of which Casy prophesied.

Al Joad

Al's role in the novel is somewhat minor. He functions as a contrast to the more serious Tom. Our first view of Al is of him swaggering home after "tom-cattin'" all night. And throughout the novel his main concern is finding a girl and in working on cars. He wants to leave the family from the very first and go work in some garage. When Tom is talking with Casy just before Casy is murdered, Tom tells Casy that Al wouldn't quit work for the sake of a strike or for any cause, and that Al's only interest is in finding some girl.

Jim Casy

It seems as though Steinbeck created in Jim Casy a modern Christ-figure but without the Christian doctrine. The initials of his name, J. C., are the same as Jesus Christ. He was a preacher, who traveled about the country preaching but refusing to take up a collection. He was quite content to preach for a meal or for a pair of shoes or some item of clothing. Then he disappeared and went into the wilderness in order to think things out. When he reappears in the first of the novel, he has not yet solved all of his problems. He is working toward an Emersonian doctrine of the Oversoul. Tom recalls that "one time Casy went into the wilderness to find his own soul, an' he foun' he didn't have no soul that was his'n. Says he foun' he jus' got a little piece of a great big soul...his little piece of a soul wasn't no good 'less it was with the rest, an' was whole." In its broadest view, this is part of Emerson's view of the Oversoul, that is, man's soul is breaking away from some larger soul and in death this individual soul is reunited with the larger Oversoul. Therefore, Casy sees good in all things and good in all people. And he feels a kinship with all people because all people have come from the same essential source and will return there. Consequently, he views all acts as good and holy. Eating, drinking, talking, fornicating, cussing, and all things are holy because they are done by men and man himself is holy.

It is not until he is put in prison after he sacrificed himself for Tom that Casy is able to come to a full understanding of his views. Here in prison, he sees the advantage of men organizing and working together to achieve some goal. He leaves the prison and tries to put his thoughts and ideas into action. But again, like Christ, he aroused the antagonism of the people in authority and was brutally slain. He died, like Christ, saying to his crucifiers: you don't know what you are doing. And it is only after his death that the full meaning of his message reaches people and he has followers or disciples. Certainly Tom must be seen as a disciple of Casy.

Casy's function in the novel is to offer the social message, and to react with the Joads. Without Casy's ideas, it would be difficult for Tom to reach the point of development that he achieves. And Casy's ideas are seen in action in many of Ma Joad's actions.

SUGGESTED EXAMINATION QUESTIONS

1. What importance is attached to Tom's having been in prison? (See *commentary* after Chapters II, IV, and XXVIII.)

2. How does Muley Graves function in the novel? (See *commentary* after Chapter VI.)

3. Why has Jim Casy ceased being a preacher? (See *commentary* after Chapter IV.)

4. What is Casy's view of life now? (See *commentaries* after Chapters IV, XXVIII, and the Character Analysis of Casy.)

5. What is the purpose of the intercalary chapters? (See section on structure and the *commentary* after each individual intercalary chapter.)

6. What is the purpose of Grampa's death? How is it correlated with the adoption of the Wilsons? (See *commentary* after Chapter XIII and the section on The General Meaning of *The Grapes of Wrath*.)

7. Describe the Joad's arrival in California. (See *commentaries* after Chapters XVIII, XX, and XXI.)

8. How is Casy's change from a man of thought to a man of action brought about? (See *commentary* after Chapter XX.)

9. How is the economic plight of the Joads correlated with the breakup of the family? (See Chapters XX, XXVIII, and the section on Structure.)

SELECTED BIBLIOGRAPHY

BLOOM, HAROLD, ed. *John Steinbeck's* The Grapes of Wrath. New York: Chelsea House, 1988.

COOK, SYLVIA. "Steinbeck, the People, and the Party." *Steinbeck Quarterly* 15 (1982): 11–23.

DAVIS, ROBERT CON, ed. *Twentieth Century Interpretations of* The Grapes of Wrath. Englewood Cliffs, New Jersey: Prentice-Hall, 1982.

DAVIS, ROBERT MURRAY. "The World of John Steinbeck's Joads." *World Literature Today* 64.3 (1990): 401–04.

DEMOTT, ROBERT. "'Working Days and Hours': Steinbeck's Writing of *The Grapes of Wrath.*" *Studies in American Fiction* 18.1 (1990): 3–15.

DIRCKS, PHYLLIS T. "Steinbeck's Statement on the Inner Chapters of *The Grapes of Wrath.*" *Steinbeck Quarterly* 24 (1991): 86–94.

DITSKY, JOHN, ed. *Critical Essays on Steinbeck's* The Grapes of Wrath. Boston: G. K. Hall, 1989.

DONOHUE, AGNES MCNEILL, ed. *A Casebook on* The Grapes of Wrath. New York: Thomas Y. Crowell, 1968.

FRENCH, WARREN, ed. *A Companion to* The Grapes of Wrath. New York: Viking Press, 1963.

GARCIA, RELOY. "The Rocky Road to Eldorado: The Journey Motif in John Steinbeck's *The Grapes of Wrath.*" *Steinbeck Quarterly* 14 (1981): 83–93.

HAYASHI, TETSUMARO, ed. *John Steinbeck: The Years of Greatness, 1936–1939.* Tuscaloosa: University of Alabama Press, 1993.

_____. *Steinbeck's* The Grapes of Wrath: *Essays in Criticism*. Muncie, Indiana: Steinbeck Research Institute, 1990.

HEAVILIN, BARBARA ANNE. "Hospitality, the Joads, and the Stranger Motif: Structural Symmetry in John Steinbeck's *The Grapes of Wrath.*" *South Dakota Review* 29.2 (1991): 142–52.

McCARTHY, PAUL EUGENE. "The Joads and Other Rural Families in Depression Fiction." *South Dakota Review* 19.3 (1981): 51–68.

MOTLEY, WARREN. "From Patriarchy to Matriarchy: Ma Joad's Role in *The Grapes of Wrath.*" *American Literature* 54.3 (1982): 397–412.

PRESSMAN, RICHARD S. "'Them's Horses—We're Men': Social Tendency in *The Grapes of Wrath.*" *Steinbeck Quarterly* 19 (1986): 71–79.

ROMBOLD, TAMARA. "Biblical Inversion in *The Grapes of Wrath.*" *College Literature* 14.2 (1987): 146–66.

TIMMERMAN, JOHN H. "The Squatter's Circle in *The Grapes of Wrath.*" *Studies in American Fiction* 17.2 (1989): 203–11.

VISSER, NICHOLAS. "Audience and Closure in *The Grapes of Wrath.*" *Studies in American Fiction* 22.1 (1994): 19–36.

WERLOCK, ABBY. "Poor Whites: Joads and Snopeses." *San Jose Studies* 18.1 (1992): 61–71.

WYATT, DAVID, ed. *New Essays on* The Grapes of Wrath. Cambridge: Cambridge University Press, 1990.

Your Guides to Successful Test Preparation.

Cliffs Test Preparation Guides

• Complete • Concise • Functional • In-depth

Efficient preparation means better test scores. Go with the experts and use *Cliffs Test Preparation Guides*. They focus on helping you know what to expect from each test, and their test-taking techniques have been proven in classroom programs nationwide. Recommended for individual use or as a part of a formal test preparation program.

Publisher's ISBN Prefix 0-8220

Qty.	ISBN	Title	Price	Qty.	ISBN	Title	Price
	2078-5	ACT	8.95		2044-0	Police Sergeant Exam	9.95
	2069-6	CBEST	8.95		2047-5	Police Officer Exam	14.95
	2056-4	CLAST	9.95		2049-1	Police Management Exam	17.95
	2071-8	ELM Review	8.95		2076-9	Praxis I: PPST	9.95
	2077-7	GED	11.95		2017-3	Praxis II: NTE Core Battery	14.95
	2061-0	GMAT	9.95		2074-2	SAT*	9.95
	2073-4	GRE	9.95		2325-3	SAT II*	14.95
	2066-1	LSAT	9.95		2072-6	TASP	8.95
	2046-7	MAT	12.95		2079-3	TOEFL w/cassettes	29.95
	2033-5	Math Review	8.95		2080-7	TOEFL Adv. Prac. (w/cass.)	24.95
	2048-3	MSAT	24.95		2034-3	Verbal Review	7.95
	2020-3	Memory Power for Exams	5.95		2043-2	Writing Proficiency Exam	8.95

Prices subject to change without notice.

Available at your booksellers, or send this form with your check or money order to **Cliffs Notes, Inc.,** P.O. Box 80728, Lincoln, NE 68501 http://www.cliffs.com

☐ Money order ☐ Check payable to Cliffs Notes, Inc.

☐ Visa ☐ Mastercard Signature_____

Card no. _____ Exp. date_____

Signature _____

Name _____

Address _____

City _____ State_____ Zip_____

*GRE, MSAT, Praxis PPST, NTE, TOEFL and Adv. Practice are registered trademarks of ETS. SAT is a registered trademark of CEEB.

Think Quick

Now there are more Cliffs Quick Review® titles, providing help with more introductory level courses. Use Quick Reviews to increase your understanding of fundamental principles in a given subject, as well as to prepare for quizzes, midterms and finals.

Do better in the classroom, and on papers and tests with Cliffs Quick Reviews.